Preserving Everything

THE COUNTRYMAN PRESS · VT. · WOODSTOCK

Preserving Everything

How to Can, Culture, Pickle, Freeze, Ferment, Dehydrate, Salt, Smoke, and Store Fruits, Vegetables, Meat, Milk, and More

LEDA MEREDITH

Preserving Everything

ISBN 978-1-58157242-1

Published by

THE COUNTRYMAN PRESS

P.O. Box 748, Woodstock, VT 05091

Distributed by

W. W. NORTON & COMPANY, INC

500 Fifth Avenue, New York, NY 10110

Printed in the United States

10 9 8 7 6 5 4 3 2 1

CONTENTS

Introduction 8

Gear 10

Troubleshooting 252

Appendix: Approximate
pH Values of Various Foods 259

Useful Resources 262

Index 265

Acknowledgments 271

About the Author 272

LACTO-FERMENTATION 21

BOILING WATER BATH CANNING 48

VINEGAR PICKLING 64

SWEET PRESERVES 88

PRESSURE CANNING 120

DEHYDRATING 140

SALTING AND SMOKING 168

FREEZING 184

COLD STORAGE 194

DAIRY CULTURES—YOGURT AND
SIMPLE CHEESES 206

PRESERVING IN OIL, BUTTER,
AND OTHER FATS 221

PRESERVING IN ALCOHOL 237

The 21st-Century Pantry

Preserving Everything is a pretty audacious title: How can I claim to write a book that covers preserving every ingredient in existence? Here's the deal: By the time you finish reading this book, not only will you have read through and hopefully tried a few recipes, but you'll also understand the method behind the recipes and be able to apply those methods, safely and deliciously, to other ingredients and recipes. I'm going to teach you the different techniques of food preservation, what it is about them that safely preserves food, and how to use them to preserve every type of food. So yes, this is a book on preserving everything!

Even in this age of take-out dinners and miniature kitchens, people rely upon food preservation whether they realize it or not. Those raisins you tuck into your kid's lunchbox are a dehydrated fruit, that jar of pasta sauce was pressure canned, and—if it's the real deal—the dill pickle that came with your deli sandwich was lacto-fermented.

In the 21st century, food preservation is more than a way to stock up for the winter, save on the grocery bill, or make some cute food gifts for the holidays. Although it can certainly be all of those things, contemporary food preservation is also a way to reduce your carbon footprint by having locally grown or raised foods on hand year-round. Think about it: How much more fossil fuel gets burned trucking commercial canned tomatoes to you across thousands of miles versus canning your own using tomatoes from your garden or your local farmers' markets?

You will find delicious recipes in this book that demonstrate each of the different food preservation techniques. There are must-have pantry basics like canned tomatoes and strawberry jam, but also more playful inventions such as fig jam with wine and balsamic vinegar. In other words, there's something here for novices and experienced food preservationists alike.

And at every step of the way you will understand exactly which component of each recipe is safely preserving the food. Is it the acidity of vinegar, the hotter-than-boiling-water heat of pressure canning, or some other factor? With this book in hand, you won't have to guess: You'll know exactly why the recipe works, and you'll even be able to invent your own food preservation recipes with absolute confidence.

I know, I know, I'm not supposed to say that. Most food preservation advice absolutely prohibits experimentation. I understand why: Food safety is a life-and-death issue. But instead of scaring folks away and restricting access to knowledge with a do-not-attempt approach, I'd rather teach you to be your own expert.

And I do mean expert. Here's the deal: There are some very straightforward food safety necessities that accompany each method of food preservation. These are essential to follow precisely. They are also very easy to follow and to learn. Once you understand what it is about each food preservation method that enables it to preserve food safely, you'll know exactly what you can and cannot change about a recipe (in this book or from any other source).

Understanding what makes each method work will also enable you to traverse the wealth of online recipes safely and successfully. There are some excellent recipes out there, but there are also some dubious ones that I would not risk feeding to myself or family. With this book in hand, you'll be able to tell at a glance whether a food preservation recipe is trustworthy.

There is a primal satisfaction that comes from looking at a batch of food you put up yourself. Anyone who has ever smiled when they heard a canning lid seal with an unmistakable pop, or tried to look modest when an appreciative gift recipient gasped, "You made this?" knows exactly what I am talking about. And now it's your turn.

Generally Useful Gear

In addition to basic kitchen equipment like mixing bowls, colanders, pots, knives, and stirring spoons, each food preservation method has a few pieces of special gear that are either essential or that make the job much easier than it would be otherwise. But first, here is some gear that you may want to get if you don't already own it. These items will be useful for many, many food preservation projects. None of them is required to make the recipes in this book, but they will make your job easier.

Generally Useful Gear

CHERRY PITTER

If you want to make the Fermented Sour Cherries in the Preserving in Alcohol chapter—or any other cherry preserve—a cherry pitter makes the job so much easier. You can also use an olive pitter. Either one is an inexpensive handheld tool that pops out each cherry (or olive) pit in a second.

A FOOD PROCESSOR

Not mandatory if you don't mind a lot of knife work, but, really helpful for recipes that require fairly large quantities of fresh ingredients to be chopped very small (the Sweet Red Pepper and Cucumber Relish recipe in the Vinegar Pickling chapter comes to mind).

KITCHEN SCALE

Top of the line is a digital scale that can handle large quantities (pounds/kilos) and also accurately

measure small amounts (ounces/grams). If you go with non-digital, you may want to invest in two pieces of gear for weighing—one to handle the heavier items and a smaller, postal-type scale for more delicate measurements.

MANDOLINE

A mandoline is a hand-powered tool that comes with several different slicing options. You can use it to quickly julienne root vegetables or fruit into matchstick-sized slivers, or to cut them into thin rounds. Think of it as a food processor that uses your arm movement instead of electricity. Warning: This is a wickedly sharp gadget, and there's a reason it comes with something called a "hand guard." Use the guard.

MORTAR AND PESTLE

Freshly ground or lightly crushed spices have unique aromas and flavors that can't be duplicated by their pre-ground counterparts. Sure, you could use an electric coffee grinder instead of the mortar and pestle. But the pulverized result won't have the same wonderfully aromatic quality as the seeds you crush the old-fashioned way. If you don't have a mortar and pestle, you can improvise with a roundish rock that you roll over the spices on a flat rock—you'll still get better results than you would with an electric grinder.

SLOTTED SPOON

Especially useful for hot pack recipes in which the food is cooked and then transferred to the jars before the canning liquid is poured over the other ingredients. But there are many other types of recipes in this

and other food preservation books that call for this piece of gear.

In addition to generally useful gear, there are tools specific to each food preservation technique that you'll want to have. See Useful Resources at the back of this book for where to order the following gear if you can't find it near you.

Gear for Lacto-Fermentation

WIDEMOUTH GLASS JARS

You don't need special canning jars for lacto-fermentation since it's best not to heat-process probiotic foods, but I do recommend that you use glass rather than plastic. Using jars with wide rather than narrow openings makes it easier to pack in the ingredients, especially with recipes such as sauerkraut for which you need to be able to press down directly on the food in the jar.

CERAMIC CROCK

This is optional, but handy if you want to make batches of a ferment that are larger than a single quart jar holds. Crocks are ceramic cylinders, taller than they are wide. They may be as simple as a vessel and lid, or slightly more complicated. Fancier models such as the Schmitt Fermenting Crock Pot (highly recommended) have rims that allow for a moat of water that seals out molds and other potentially harmful microorganisms while allowing the gases produced by fermentation to escape. They also come with fitted weights.

WEIGHT TO FIT INSIDE CROCK

If you are making a large batch of a ferment and you don't have a crock that came with a custom-fit weight, then you will need to make one. Its purpose is to keep the solid food submerged beneath the liquid brine. No need to spend money or go high tech with this: A plate that fits inside the crock, weighted with a closed jar that is filled with water and placed on top of the plate, works fine.

Many fermentation practitioners recommend using a sealed, plastic Ziploc bag filled with brine as a weight. Brine is used instead of water as a precaution in case the bag leaks—plain water would dilute the brine. This method certainly works, but I am not a fan because the plastic is in direct contact with the food.

Gear for Boiling Water Bath Canning, Pressure Canning, Sweet Preserves, and Vinegar Pickling

These food preservation methods will all be much easier if you have the following equipment.

CANNING FUNNEL

This is a funnel with a much wider hole at the bottom than the usual narrow funnel aperture. It is not absolutely essential gear, but will save you much kitchen mess when you transfer piping-hot food into canning jars. It is also useful for tasks such as pouring rice or other dry bulk foods into jars. Every kitchen should have one.

CANNING JARS AND LIDS

Canning jars are made of heatproof glass that can withstand the high temperatures of a boiling water bath or pressure canning. They are made to fit with either widemouth or "regular"-sized canning lids. For home canning, quart or single-liter jars are the largest practical size, with the smallest being 4 ounces.

The necks of most canning jars are made for the two sizes of lids mentioned (the smallest Quattro Stagioni lids are an exception, and you cannot use any other brand of lid with them). Most are two-piece lids that have a disk with an adhesive ring on the underside, and a screw-on ring that holds the disk in place during the canning process. There are also brands of canning lids that are a single piece, again with the adhesive ring on the underside. And there are reusable

canning lids that have a separate rubber ring.

When you buy new canning jars, they will come with canning lids. Note that although the screw-on rings of two-piece lids may be reused, the inner disks should not be because the adhesive ring wears out and the lids can fail to seal. This applies to the adhesive on single-piece lids as well (single-piece canning lids should only be reused for food storage, not for repeat canning). An exception to the rule about not reusing the inner ring of canning lids is the Tattler brand of reusable lids (see Useful Resources).

Notice that I am not mentioning the old-fashioned glass lid clamp-down jars with the rubber ring, still sold in many places. These are fantastic for ferments and storing dehydrated and salted foods. They are much less reliable than the canning jars described above for canning, however, and it is harder to confirm a successful seal with them.

JAR LIFTER

This tool makes it easy to move hot jars into and out of the canner, and to carry them to their cooling-off location. You will be especially grateful to have one of these when you need to remove entirely submerged jars from the steaming water of a boiling water bath.

LID LIFTER

When you sterilize jars for canning, you put the lids into the hot water after you have finished boiling the glass jars. Then you have to get them back out again. That can be tricky, especially with the flat disks of two-piece canning lids. A lid lifter is a gadget that turns it into an easy task. There are two models. One is a rack that holds the lids and has a tall handle sticking up above the surface of the water. The other is a stick with a magnet on the end; this type only works with metal canning lids, not the reuseable plastic models.

pH METER

This gadget is entirely optional if you are using the recipes in this book because these recipes have already had their pH tested. But if you want to start experimenting with your own canning recipes, this is the tool that will let you know whether what you have made is acidic enough to be safely canned in a boiling water bath, or if it must be pressure canned. That information is the main difference between safe and dangerous canning practices.

The best pH meters use an electrode that is immersed in the food and gives you an accurate digital reading of the pH of your recipe. Food with a pH of 4.6 or lower can go into a boiling water bath; a higher pH reading means you need to get out the pressure canner.

See Useful Resources for where to get pH meters.

ROUND RACK

This fits inside your pressure canner or boiling water bath pot and prevents the glass jars from cracking during processing. All new pressure canners come with custom-fitted racks. For boiling water baths, especially if you're improvising one by using a non-canner-specific vessel such as a stockpot, you can use a round cake rack.

Gear for Boiling Water Bath Canning

DEEP POT

For boiling water bath canning, the jars of food must be fully immersed with 1 to 2 inches of water above the lids. It is not necessary to purchase a special canner for boiling water bath canning, but the one you use must be deep enough. Soup stockpots work well because of their depth. For small jars (half- or quarter-pint), you can use one of those pasta pots that comes with a built-in rack. A pressure canner can also double as a boiling water bath (instructions for that are in the Pressure Canning chapter).

Gear for Vinegar Pickling

ACID TITRATION TEST KIT

Not essential unless you plan to use homemade vinegar for pickling. This inexpensive kit, available from home winemaking suppliers (see Useful Resources), enables you to test your homemade vinegar to see if it has a high enough percentage of acetic acid to replace commercially sold vinegar in pickle recipes.

Gear for Sweet Preserves

JELLY BAG

A jelly bag makes the difference between a cloudy jelly and a gorgeously translucent one. It can also be used for straining juices and syrups. You can buy jelly bags that come with their own stands for suspending them

over a bowl or pot, or you can rig your own stand by suspending a colander above a large bowl or pot: Place a rack or a couple of long-handled wooden spoons across the bowl or pot, and then put the colander with the jelly bag in it on top of the rack or handles. Jelly bags are often made of synthetic material, but you can also use butter muslin or the cloth produce bags that are sold to replace plastic bags at the supermarket.

Your jelly bag can also stand in for cheesecloth in straining recipes such as labneh (yogurt cheese; see the Dairy chapter).

FOOD MILL

Not essential, but useful for separating seeds and skins from fruits and vegetables while simultaneously puréeing them. I use my food mill when I'm making applesauce, for example, which lets me skip the step of peeling the apples. If you don't have a food mill, you can try pressing the food through a colander or sieve with the back of the spoon for a similar result, but that is much more labor intensive.

Gear for Pressure Canning

WEIGHTED OR DIAL GAUGE PRESSURE CANNER

This is the essential piece of equipment for safely canning non-acidic foods. Unlike boiling water bath canning, you cannot use just any old deep pot for food that must be pressure canned. See the chapter on Pressure Canning for more details about the different types of pressure canners, and Useful Resources for where to get them.

Gear for Dehydrating

DEHYDRATOR

Not essential, since food can also be dehydrated in your oven, or even outdoors in the sun if you live in an arid enough region (or make a solar dehydrator). But an electric dehydrator is capable of maintaining lower temperatures than you can achieve in most ovens, has a fan to circulate air around the food, and uses less energy than an oven. See Useful Resources.

Gear for Salting and Smoking

The simply salt-cured recipes in this book such as pancetta and salt fish require no special equipment. But those that are smoked after they are cured do.

SMOKER

These range from basic and inexpensive homemade contraptions to fancy, and frequently pricey commercial models. See the chapter on Salting and Smoking for information on the different types of smokers.

CHARCOAL CHIMNEY

Not essential, but very useful for getting coals burning outside the smoker during long-smoked recipes. The coals are easy to start in one of these chimneys (available at most hardware stores), and you can get them to exactly the stage you want before adding the coals to the smoker as needed. This helps you to minimize fluctuations in temperature during the several hours of smoking the food.

DIGITAL MEAT THERMOMETER

This is the piece of gear that tells you what the internal temperature of your meat or fish is, letting you know when it is cooked through. Get one that has a flexible probe and a heatproof, magnetized readout: The probe is inserted into the food, while the part that gives you the temperature sits on the outside of the smoker. This means that you do not need to repeatedly open the smoker to check the internal temperature of the food. Most digital thermometers also have an alarm setting that will beep at you when the center of the food reaches the target temperature—very handy if you're busy entertaining guests at the same time you're smoking something.

Your meat thermometer can also double as a cheese-making thermometer.

Gear for Freezing

In addition to the obvious and essential freezer, the following items are useful for freezing food.

FREEZER BAGS AND/OR CONTAINERS

Regular plastic storage bags tend to be too thin to protect food from freezer burn, so if you are going to use plastic it's worth spending the bit extra they cost to buy the thicker, freezer Ziploc bags.

An advantage of using freezer-safe containers rather than bags is that you can choose ones that are BPA-free. These are usually made either of stainless steel or thick glass that won't crack in the freezer. You can also freeze food in some canning jars. Only use widemouth canning jars for this purpose, the ones

with straight sides (no narrowing at the neck). With all containers, be sure to leave some head space since the water in the food will expand as it freezes.

BUTCHER PAPER

This is the best option for wrapping meat, poultry, and fish destined for the freezer. You can get butcher paper from online suppliers (see Useful Resources), or even from office supply stores (where it will be near school craft supplies).

VACUUM SEALER

Food that is destined for the freezer will keep better quality and not get freezer burn as easily if it is vacuum sealed. Some dehydrated foods also benefit from being stored in vacuum-sealed bags: Kale chips, for example, keep their crunch much longer if stored this way. If you plan to dry and especially to freeze food in quantity, a tabletop vacuum sealer is a worthwhile investment. See Useful Resources.

Gear for Cold Storage

HYGROMETER

Not essential, but useful for keeping track of the humidity in a root cellar. See Useful Resources.

Gear for Simple Cheese Making

WIDEMOUTH GLASS JARS OR STAIN-LESS-STEEL CONTAINERS

If you are using glass jars, they don't have to be canning jars. But as with lacto-fermentation, I recommend staying away from plastic for cheese making.

CHEESECLOTH, BUTTER MUSLIN, OR JELLY BAG

Cheesecloth has the advantage of being widely available at supermarkets and other kitchen supply stores. But you have to use a lot of layers of cheesecloth to duplicate the fine straining action of butter muslin or a jelly bag. It also isn't as easy to rinse out and reuse cheesecloth as it is butter muslin or jelly bags. See Useful Resources for mail-order sources of butter muslin and jelly bags.

THERMOMETER

You can certainly use a digital meat thermometer such as the one I recommended for smoking meat and fish. But there are non-electric food thermometers that also work just fine for cheese making.

Gear for Preserving in Alcohol

FERMENTATION LOCK

A fermentation lock has one end that looks something like a plastic cork and another end that is a plastic contraption you partially fill with water. It allows the gases produced by fermentation to escape while simultaneously keeping out molds and bacteria. Fermentation lock sizes range from those that will fit into a repurposed wine bottle to those meant for gallon and larger carboys. They are inexpensive and available from any home winemaking supplier (see Useful Resources).

If you don't want to bother ordering a fermentation lock, you can also use a pricked balloon to achieve the same goal: Letting gases escape while keeping mold and bacteria out. See the Preserving in Alcohol chapter for instructions.

CHAPTER ONE

Lacto-fermentation

Lacto-fermentation is the process that turns cucumbers into classic deli dill pickles. It is what turns cabbage into sauerkraut, and it is the secret behind traditional Korean kimchi. It is one of the oldest forms of food preservation: Humanity has had thousands of years of experience with it. Lacto-fermented foods contain probiotics that have been credited with the longevity of centenarians in societies that eat a lot of fermented food (and can brag of a relatively high percentage of the population who live to be over 100 years old).

You have been eating fermented foods for years whether you've realized it or not. In addition to the obvious ones like wine and beer, fermented foods include soy sauce, chocolate, vinegar, bread, tea, and miso. They also include many foods commonly called "pickles," which can be confusing because vinegar-based preserves are also called pickles. But the process that makes vinegar-brined pickles is quite different from the transformation wrought by living organisms that creates a fermented pickle.

It is fascinating that of all the methods of food preservation, fermentation—especially lacto-fermentation—is the one that has had the sharpest spike in popularity in recent years. Fermentation workshops and online groups of enthusiasts abound. In an era where there are antibacterial wipes available to sanitize anything and everything before you touch it, when antibiotics are routinely administered to meat animals as a preventive rather than an emergency treatment, why are so many people nevertheless eager to eat and make foods that depend upon a thriving population of bacteria?

Maybe it is because of yogurt, which is a fermented food (I debated whether to include yogurt in this chapter rather than in the one on dairy). People know that yogurt is supposed to be good for them. Most people also know that the label claim "with live acidophilus cultures" means something especially healthy, even if they aren't sure exactly what. Perhaps they had been paying steep prices for "probiotics" at the health food store to keep their digestive and immune systems healthy, reduce inflammation, speed recovery from yeast infections, and possibly even prevent certain forms of cancer. Then they found out that they could be getting those same healthy probiotics cheaply and deliciously by fermenting foods at home. In these microbe-phobic times, *live cultures* and *probiotics* are polite ways to describe the bacterial frenzy that creates lacto-fermented food.

How Lacto-Fermentation Safely Preserves Food

Take some chopped-up vegetables and put them in a jar (it doesn't have to be sterilized). Cover them with a mildly salty brine. Leave them out at room temperature for a few days or weeks then transfer them to a cool but not freezing place. That is basically the entire technique of lacto-fermentation.

To many people, that process sounds completely counterintuitive and scary. You *don't* have to sterilize the jars? And you leave the food out *at room temperature*, not just for an hour or two but for days? And you do *not* blast away bacteria with high heat by canning the food? Here's how it works, and why it's safe.

Among the many different bacteria we share the planet with, there are some that can be dangerous, even lethal to us (hello, botulism toxin). But there are also others that not only do not harm us but actually make us healthier. Indeed, current research shows that we couldn't live without the beneficial bacteria that are always there inside us, living in intricate relationships with our bodies.

At its most basic level, lacto-fermentation works because it creates extreme pH environments. The process relies upon several salt-tolerant bacteria species within the genus *Lactobacillus*. These good-guy bacteria exist on the surface of vegetables and fruits. In most lacto-fermentation recipes, the fresh food is covered in a salty (alkaline) brine. The salty brine begins the elimination of harmful bacteria that are not as salt tolerant as *Lactobacillus*, and encourages the latter to start fermenting the food. During the fermentation, the *Lactobacillus* convert lactose and other sugars in the food into lactic acid. That's why the process is called *lacto*-fermentation. The lactic acid creates a low-pH (acidic) environment that harmful bacteria cannot survive in (and the lactic acid is also what gives lacto-fermented foods their characteristically tangy taste). Basically, the probiotic bacteria take over the neighborhood and make it inhospitable to other bacteria.

What to Expect During Fermentation

Within a day or two at room temperature, you'll start to see some bubbles on the surface of the brine the food is submerged in. The liquid will change from clear to having a slightly cloudier appearance (but it should *not* be completely cloudy). It will develop a pleasantly light, sour smell (think pickles).

Once these changes signal that fermentation is under way, you will transfer your ferment to someplace colder than room temperature, such as your refrigerator. Fermentation will continue, but it will be greatly slowed by the colder temperature. This means that your fermented foods keep their texture longer than they would if they continued to ferment quickly at warm temperatures. This is especially important when crispness is part of the culinary profile of the food, as it should be with sauerkraut or fermented radishes, for example. But it also means that the sour taste of your ferments will get more so over time, even in the refrigerator or a cold cellar. If you discover that you prefer the lighter flavor of a recently made ferment, make small batches and plan on eating them within a few weeks. If you want a bolder taste, wait as long as several months before digging in.

HOW TO GET A WHEY STARTER CULTURE FROM YOGURT

When you strain plain yogurt to make either Greek yogurt or yogurt cheese (labneh; both are described in the Dairy chapter), the by-product is a yellowish, semi-clear liquid. That liquid is whey, and it is loaded with lively *Lactobacillus* probiotic bacteria.

About Starter Cultures and Fermenting Without Added Salt

There is no need to add a starter culture to your ferments, but doing so can quicken the process. It can also help ensure a successful ferment if you decide not to use any salt at all.

It is possible to lacto-ferment food without adding salt in the first stage. One way to do this is to give the healthy bacteria a head start by introducing a starter culture. Keep in mind that even if you don't use any salt, a starter culture may not be needed—the fresh food itself will bring plenty of probiotic *Lactobacillus* bacteria to the party. But if you are leaving out salt, the extra probiotics introduced by a starter culture will slant the odds in favor of a successful fermentation.

A starter culture is simply a bit of liquid or food already teeming with healthy *Lactobacillus* bacteria. You can make your own starter either by saving a spoonful of the liquid from a previous ferment, or by making whey from yogurt. To use your starter culture, just add some to your next lacto-fermentation project. I use about a tablespoon of starter culture per pint of water or brine.

There are a few foods that I have successfully fermented using neither salt nor a starter culture, just plain filtered water. Certain vegetables work better with this method than others. Two that consistently ferment well in plain filtered water are celery and the ribs (leafstalks) of chard.

Temperature impacts salt-free lacto-fermentation even more than it does with salt-added brines. Salt-free ferments tend to spoil when the room temperature climbs over 85°F.

WHY NOT JUST USE TAP WATER?

Most municipal water is chlorinated, and that chlorine is added specifically for the purpose of killing off bacteria. It does such a powerful job that it can kill off the probiotic *Lactobacillus* bacteria you are counting on to ferment your recipe.

Tips for Successful Lacto-Fermentation

- The hotter the environment, the more salt you need in your initial brine. In warm environments, the food can spoil before the beneficial bacteria have a chance to establish a good ferment. This is why it is easier to ferment foods in cool weather, and one of the reasons why ferments are often made with cool-weather crops such as cabbage and root vegetables. Salt-free ferments can be especially tricky in hot weather. If you're hoping to make crisp fermented pickles in the warmest weeks of summer, it's wise to add a little extra salt to the brine.

- Use vegetables and fruits that are in excellent condition. You can't expect crunch from your fermented cucumbers if they were limp to begin with.

- Remember to always use filtered or non-chlorinated water.

- Once you start eating out of one of your jars or crocks of lacto-fermented food, be prepared to do a little maintenance work. Anytime a container gets down to two-thirds or less of its lacto-fermented contents, it is a good idea to transfer the remaining goods to a smaller jar or container. Fermented food sitting in a container with a lot of air space above it tends to lift up out of the liquid that is preserving it and discolor unattractively.

- Use glass, ceramic, or stainless-steel containers for your ferments. Not only can plastic give the food an off flavor, but certain types of plastic can leach harmful compounds into the food as well.

- Eat your ferments young if you prefer a lighter flavor; let them age for a few months if you want a more mouth-puckeringly sour taste. The food will be safe for a year or longer, but even the crunchiest fermented vegetables and fruits start to soften after about 6 months.

- Store ferments you expect to eat within a few weeks on the comparatively warm shelves of the door of your refrigerator. If you want the ferment to last for months, keep good texture, and not develop an overly strong sour taste, store it on the top shelf of the main body of the refrigerator, which is the coldest area.

- Save the leftover brine after you finish eating the food it was preserving. Use it in salad dressings, or sprinkle it on lentil or bean soups. You can also use a splash of brine from a previous ferment as a starter culture to kick-start your next one.

- Canning lacto-fermented food in a boiling water bath or pressure canner is a lousy idea. It's not that you couldn't: It would be perfectly safe, and you would end up with a product closer to the canned sauerkraut at the store (although that was probably made as a vinegar-based recipe, not by traditional fermentation). What's wrong with that? The heat of the canning process will destroy all of the good-for-you probiotic bacteria in your fermented product. It will still be edible. It may even still be somewhat tasty. But you will have wiped out one of the major advantages of eating fermented foods, which is their health benefits.

Using Lacto-Fermented Foods in Cooked Recipes

Because the healthy probiotics in your ferments will be partially or wholly destroyed by high heat, try to add them to recipes at the end of the cooking time, after the heat has been turned off. For example, in Provence, lacto-fermented green bean soup is a traditional dish. First potatoes and a little garlic are added to chicken or vegetable stock over high heat. Only after the potatoes are fully cooked and the pot is removed from the heat are the green beans added. The fermented green beans warm up quickly in the soup, but are not boiled and so retain some of their probiotic health benefits.

If you plan on adding fermented vegetables to any hot dish, not just soup, chop the vegetables slightly smaller than usual so that they warm through easily without needing to be cooked. Fortunately, lacto-fermented vegetables don't need to cook as long as unfermented vegetables in order to get tender.

If you have a strong craving for piping-hot sauerkraut alongside your sausage (as they eat it in several northern European countries), go for it. But know that although it may taste great steaming hot, it doesn't have the health perks that the uncooked version does.

More Lacto-Fermentation Recipes

These recipes are in single-jar or small-batch amounts because those are the most practical for many people nowadays. But if you want to do bigger batches, by all means, go for it. Just keep in mind that when you are using a crock or other widemouth vessel to ferment your recipe in, you will need some kind of weight to keep the ingredients from floating up out of the brine. Some specialized fermenting crocks included fitted weights for this purpose, but you can improvise something that works just as well by putting a plate that is small enough to fit inside the crock (but still large enough to cover most of the food) on top of the ingredients. Weight the plate by putting a closed jar of water on top of it. You could also use a brick or stone, so long as you sterilized these before using them as weights (they will be in contact with the brine, and therefore with your fermenting food).

I've seen instructions that recommend using a plastic bag filled with salt brine as a weight, and I admit to having used that method in the past. The reason for using salt brine instead of plain water is that if the bag leaks, the fermentation's salt brine will not be diluted. As a weight for keeping ingredients submerged in liquid, this technique works just fine. But with an ever-increasing number of people (including myself) trying to move away from using plastic, I no longer recommend it.

Fermented Chard

PREP TIME: 5 minutes   INITIAL FERMENTATION TIME: 24–72 hours
YIELD: 1 pint; recipe can be multiplied

You can't get any simpler than this two-ingredient ferment! It's a nice introduction to the fermentation process.

Chard—also known as Swiss chard (except in Switzerland, where they find it amusing that we call it that)—is a leafy green that I treat as two different vegetables. There is the green part, which is excellent raw or cooked. And then there are the thick, juicy, crisp leafstalks. The latter is what we will use to make this ferment.

You can use any variety for this ferment. Rainbow chard with its red, gold, and white leafstalks makes an attractive and festive-looking ferment, but the plain white variety tastes just as good.

Beets are actually the same species as chard (*Beta vulgaris*), so if you have some beet greens feel free to use those leafstalks instead.

Lacto-fermented chard ribs are good on top of salads, but also added at the last minute to soups. They are excellent baked into casseroles with chickpeas and feta cheese, if you don't mind losing some of the probiotic benefits to the oven heat.

INGREDIENTS

Leafstalks from 1 large bunch of chard leaves

Filtered or non-chlorinated water

INSTRUCTIONS

1. Wash the chard leaves and slice off the green parts (save those for another use). Chop the chard leafstalks into ½- or 1-inch pieces.

2. Pack the chard into a clean glass jar. Set the jar on a small plate. Pour the filtered or non-chlorinated water over the chard pieces. Fill the jar all the way to the rim, then place a lid on top. The lid will keep the chard pieces submerged in the water, but you want it on loosely enough that gases can escape during fermentation.

3. Leave the jar of chard at room temperature for 24 hours. After that, take off the lid and check for signs of fermentation. Within 24 to 72 hours you should see some bubbles or foam on the surface of the liquid, and the chard will start to have the characteristic light sour smell of a fresh fermentation. Leave the chard at room temperature until it is clearly fermenting. During the 1 to 3 days that this will take, keep the jar topped up with filtered or non-chlorinated water at all times.

4. Once fermentation has been under way for a couple of days, pour out just a tiny bit of the liquid and seal the lid tightly this time. Put the lacto-fermented chard into the refrigerator or a cold cellar. It will keep, chilled, for at least 6 months, but the texture is best if it is eaten within 3 months. Note that white chard leafstalks sometimes darken when they are fermented, especially the pieces in the top half of the jar. This is harmless, and they will still taste good.

Single-Jar Sauerkraut

PREP TIME: 5 minutes   SALTING TIME: 4 hours   INITIAL FERMENTATION TIME: 2–3 days   YIELD: 1 quart

---

There is good reason why for fermentation guru Sandor Ellix Katz calls sauerkraut "the gateway ferment." People who would otherwise back away from the combination of lively bacterial action and raw food calm down when told, "That's how sauerkraut is made." They've eaten sauerkraut, maybe on a hot dog; it's a familiar food. And the recipe is undauntingly simple, just cabbage and salt (plus optional seasonings: Caraway and juniper berries are traditional).

If you don't think you are a sauerkraut fan, you might want to give the home-made version a chance. Especially when it has been recently made, it has a much lighter taste than the vinegar-based, canned commercial versions.

Sauerkraut will keep in the refrigerator for at least 6 months, but it is best if eaten within 3 months because the cabbage starts to lose its texture after that. It will keep longest if stored on the top shelf of the main compartment because that is the coldest part of refrigerators (more about that in the Cold Storage chapter).

INGREDIENTS

1 small red or white cabbage

1–2 tablespoons kosher or sea salt

¼ teaspoon caraway seeds (optional)

3–6 juniper berries (optional)

INSTRUCTIONS

1. Cut the small cabbage in half and then slice out the tough core and stem. Slice the remaining cabbage into thin ribbons or small pieces.

2. Pack the cabbage into a clean, widemouth glass jar. Sprinkle the cabbage with the salt as you add it to the jar. Also add the caraway seeds and juniper berries as you go. Press down on the cabbage quite firmly to start releasing its juices.

3. Cover the kraut-in-progress and let it sit at room temperature for up to 4 hours. During this time the salt should draw enough juice out of the cabbage that the vegetable pieces are completely under the liquid (you may have to press down on the kraut again to make this happen). If there is not enough cabbage juice to completely cover the food, make a brine by dissolving 2 teaspoons of kosher or sea salt in a pint of filtered or non-chlorinated water. Add the brine to the jar until the cabbage is completely submerged.

4. With larger crocks and jars, it is necessary to put a weight on ferments to keep the food submerged in the liquid. With a small single-jar recipe like this, all you need to do is fill the jar all the way to the rim with the brine. Then place the jar on a small plate or tray and loosely cover it with a lid. Because the ingredients are packed in to the brim, the lid will keep them under the brine. The plate or tray will catch any overflow that happens during the fermentation.

5. Keep the jar at room temperature for about 3 days. At least once a day, take off the lid and check on your sauerkraut. The cabbage should still be covered by the liquid. If it is not, make a brine by dissolving 1 to 2 teaspoons of kosher or sea salt in a pint of filtered or non-chlorinated water; add enough to cover the kraut. Press down on the cabbage with the back of a spoon or your clean fingers to get the pieces beneath the liquid.

    Once fermentation begins, you will see some bubbles froth up on the surface of the liquid (especially immediately after you press down on the cabbage). The kraut will start to develop its characteristic sour-but-clean taste and smell.

    Remember that temperature affects the speed of fermentation: In a cool environment, you may need to wait an extra day or so for fermentation to kick in, whereas if it's very warm the kraut may be ready for the next step after just 2 days.

6. Once fermentation has been under way for at least a couple of days, transfer the jar of sauerkraut to the refrigerator. There is no need to keep a plate under it at this point. Wait another week for the flavor of the sauerkraut to develop before eating it. The flavor will get increasingly sour as the kraut ages (remember that refrigeration slows fermentation, but does not halt it).

Radish Kimchi

PREP TIME: 15 minutes   INITIAL FERMENTATION TIME: 2–3 days   YIELD: 1 pint; recipe can be multiplied

---

Kimchi is the pungent fermented condiment that is ubiquitous in Korean cuisine. In Korea, it is made in special kimchi pots, and sometimes buried underground during its fermentation. The weather there is usually warm, and the temperature is cooler underground. Many ingredients find their way into the kimchi pot, from fiery chile peppers to raw fish. Recipes vary from family to family.

Kimchi is fermented in very much the same way as sauerkraut, and like sauerkraut is made mostly out of cabbage. With most kimchi recipes, radish is usually a side ingredient added to the cabbage, along with strong seasonings, including a lot of garlic.

In this recipe, I've reversed the usual ratio of cabbage to radishes for a crunchier kimchi. I also suggest that instead of the traditional white daikon radish you use red-skinned Cherry Belles or pink-fleshed watermelon radishes for a more colorful result.

INGREDIENTS

3 cups filtered or non-chlorinated water

2 teaspoons kosher or medium-grain sea salt

½ teaspoon soy sauce or nam pla (fish sauce)

¾ pound radishes

¼ pound cabbage leaves, sliced into thin strips

1 small onion, peeled and sliced

2 cloves garlic, peeled and sliced

1 teaspoon grated fresh ginger root

1–2 chile peppers or ½–1 teaspoon red pepper flakes

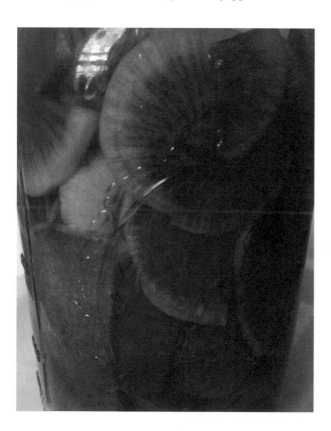

INSTRUCTIONS

1. Combine the filtered or non-chlorinated water with the salt and stir to dissolve. Stir in the soy sauce or the nam pla.

2. Wash the radishes. Slice off and compost or discard the root and stem ends. Peel large radishes such as watermelon or daikon, but leave smaller red-skinned radishes unpeeled. Slice the radishes into ⅛-inch disks, or julienne them into matchstick-sized slivers. A mandoline will make the slicing go quicker.

3. Put the radishes, cabbage, onion, garlic, ginger, and chile peppers or red pepper flakes in a large bowl and toss to combine them well. Firmly pack the vegetables and spices into a clean glass pint jar, leaving about ¼-inch head space.

4. Pour the brine over the food in the jar. Use your clean fingers or the back of a spoon to press down on the food and release any air bubbles. The brine should completely cover the vegetables and spices.

    If the food starts to float up out of the brine, you can weight it down with a smaller glass jar filled with water (set the smaller jar directly on top of the food). Or you can simply fill the jar all the way to the rim, leaving no head space at all, and then put a lid loosely on top of the jar. The lid will hold the food under the brine (remember that because you are not canning this recipe, you don't need head space in the jar to enable a vacuum seal). But don't screw the lid on tightly: You want the gases that develop during fermentation to be able to escape. Set the jar on a small plate because it will probably overflow a bit once fermentation kicks in.

5. Leave the kimchi out at room temperature for 2 to 3 days. Every day, take the lid or smaller bottle-weight off and look for signs of fermentation such as bubbles on the surface. You'll be able to see these clearly if you press down gently on the food. But don't just look for signs of fermentation: also get close with your nose and sniff for that clean but tangy pickled smell that means the safe, tasty, and healthy transformation you're after is happening. Because this is kimchi, the sour smell will also be redolent with the scent of the garlic and other seasonings.

6. When the kimchi has shown clear signs of fermenting for at least 1 day, transfer it to the refrigerator or to a cold, dark cellar. You won't need the plate under the jar any longer because the cold storage temperature will slow down fermentation so much that there shouldn't be any overflow. But you will need to remove the bottle-weight, if you used one, and replace it with the jar's lid.

NOTE

Your kimchi will be ready to eat 1 to 2 weeks after you start it, and will keep for at least a year (remember that its spicy flavor will keep getting stronger as the months go by!).

VARIATIONS

- Replace the radishes in the recipe with slivers of carrot or beet root.

- Leave out the cabbage altogether.

- Make *sauerruben* by using turnips instead of radishes.

Lacto-Fermented Green Beans

PREP TIME: 10 minutes   INITIAL FERMENTATION TIME: 1–3 days   YIELD: 1 quart

---

Green beans are one of the most popular vegetables for fermenting. Perhaps that is because of the light flavor they retain even after months in the crock or jar. Their flavor remains so mild that although you can serve them as a pickle, they are also suitable for use as a vegetable side dish.

INGREDIENTS

2 pounds green beans

3 cups filtered or non-chlorinated water

1 tablespoon kosher or medium-grain sea salt

INSTRUCTIONS

1. Wash the green beans. Slice or snap off the ends.

2. Combine the filtered or non-chlorinated water with the salt and stir to dissolve.

3. Lay a clean glass quart jar on its side and start loading in the green beans. You'll fit more beans into the jar, and they'll stand straighter, if you start by putting them in horizontally this way rather than trying to get them to stay in place with the jar vertical. Once the jar is full enough that the green beans hold one another in place, set the jar upright. Keep

stuffing in green beans until you can't fit in even one more. The beans will shrink slightly during fermentation, but packing them in very tightly keeps them from floating up out of the brine.

4. Pour the salt-and-water brine over the green beans. Make sure that they are completely covered. Put a lid on the jar, but loosely (you want the gases that develop during fermentation to be able to escape).

5. Put a small plate under the jar to catch any overflow that may occur during fermentation. Leave the jar of green beans and brine out at room temperature for 2 to 3 days. At least once a day, take the lid off and look for signs of fermentation such as bubbles on the surface. You'll see these especially if you press gently on the food. But don't just look for signs of fermentation: Also get close with your nose and sniff for that clean but tangy pickled smell that means the safe, tasty, and healthy transformation you're after is happening. Fermented green beans will smell something like a light version of sauerkraut.

6. Once the green beans have been actively fermenting for at least 24 hours, transfer them to the refrigerator or to a cool, dark cellar. You won't need the plate under the jar any longer because the cold storage temperature will slow down fermentation so much that there shouldn't be any overflow. If you put the green beans into a refrigerator, remember that the door of the fridge has a warmer temperature than the main compartment. If you want a more active fermentation to continue (and plan on eating the fermented green beans within a few weeks), store the jar on one of the shelves of the refrigerator's door. Otherwise, store them in the main compartment, preferably on the top shelf.

VARIATIONS

- Fermented yellow wax beans taste identical to green beans. I like to mix the two in a jar simply because they look attractive together.

- Add a smashed clove of garlic and/or one or two small, hot chile peppers for a spicier ferment.

- Add a sprig or two of fresh dill for an excellent flavor variation.

FIVE DELICIOUS WAYS TO
USE LACTO-FERMENTED VEGETABLES

You've turned cabbage into kraut, cucumbers into pickles, carrots into kimchi. Now what? Here are several ways to enjoy the piquant flavors of fermented foods while getting their probiotic health benefits into your diet as often as possible.

1. **Instead of Capers or Olives**
   You are cooking up a pasta sauce or a salad that calls for capers or olives, and you have neither on hand. Just chop up almost any lacto-fermented veggie into small pieces and use it instead. If you're working on a cooked sauce, add the fermented "capers" after the sauce has come off the heat so that you don't destroy the probiotics.

2. **Instead of Vinegar**
   Use the brine from a mature ferment—one that was started at least a month ago and has had time to develop plenty of sourness—instead of vinegar or lemon juice in salad dressings.

3. **In Grain Salads**
   Lacto-fermented vegetables are a great way to turn leftover cooked grains into a super-healthy quick salad that is also tasty. For two people, start with 2 cups of a cooked grain (rice, barley, quinoa, bulgur, et cetera). Mix in ½ cup chopped lacto-fermented vegetables with a little of their brine, ¼ cup minced parsley, 2 to 3 tablespoons good-quality extra-virgin olive oil, 1 to 2 tablespoons minced dill or mint, and salt to taste.

4. **Quick Winter Salad**
   This salad dresses itself thanks to the tanginess of the kraut brine. I usually make it with sauerkraut, but you could use fermented radishes or any other simple, not-too-spicy fermented vegetable. Thinly slice or julienne a crisp apple. Toss with an equal amount of sauerkraut or other thinly sliced or shredded ferment. That's already going to be good, but to make it even better add a tablespoon of sunflower seeds. And to take the salad in a different direction, mix in 1/2 to 1 teaspoon of toasted sesame oil (I know that sounds like it might be an odd combination, but trust me: It is delicious).

5. **On Your Dog . . . or Other Hot Sandwich**
   Sauerkraut on hot dogs is standard, but you can replace it with ferments that are made with vegetables other than cabbage. And you can use other kinds of meat (I'm thinking pastrami right now). There's just something so good about a hot, salty meat paired with a tangy, mildly crunchy ferment. But remember that you lose the health benefits of the ferment if you cook it. Instead, add the kraut or other ferment just before you dig in.

Fermented Hot Chile Pepper Sauce

PREP TIME: 10 minutes   FERMENTATION TIME: 3–7 days   YIELD: 1 pint

You'll never need to buy another bottle of hot sauce once you've got some of this in the house. Depending on the type of chile pepper you use, this fermented hot sauce can be wickedly fiery or just mildly spicy. The sauce is tangy from the fermentation, but with this recipe you'll taste the full flavor of the chiles as well as getting their heat.

You can puree the chile peppers and brine together for a more liquid sauce, or go for a texture closer to a relish by leaving the peppers slightly chunky.

INGREDIENTS

1 pint small, whole hot chile peppers

1 pint filtered or non-chlorinated water

1 teaspoon kosher or medium-grain sea salt

INSTRUCTIONS

1. Wash the chile peppers. Cut off the stem ends. For a very spicy sauce, leave the seeds in the peppers; for something slightly milder, slice the peppers in half lengthwise and remove the seeds and any white pith. Finely chop the peppers, or pulse them briefly in a food processor.

It's a good idea to wear rubber or plastic gloves when you're working with hot chile peppers. I never do; then again, I frequently squint my way through the next step because I accidentally rub my eyes after chopping the peppers. Don't say I didn't warn you.

2. Dissolve the salt in the water (remember to use non-chlorinated water).

3. Put the chopped chile peppers into a clean jar or jars. As with all the lacto-fermentation recipes in this chapter, it is not necessary to sterilize the jars first, but they should be scrupulously clean. Leave about ½ inch of head space. Put the jar onto a small plate to catch any overflow that occurs during fermentation.

4. Pour the salt brine over the chile peppers. Press down lightly on the peppers with the back of a spoon to release any air bubbles. Be sure the brine comes all the way up to the rim of the jar. Loosely cover the jar with a lid (do not screw it on tightly; you want the gases produced by fermentation to be able to escape).

    Alternatively, if you want a smoother, more liquid sauce, puree the chile peppers together with the brine in a blender or food processor before pouring the mixture into a jar. As with the chunkier version, place the jar on a small plate to catch overflow and loosely cover the jar with a lid.

5. Let the peppers soak in the brine at room temperature for at least 3 days but as long as 1 week. At least once a day, remove the lid and look for signs that the peppers are fermenting. Press down on them lightly with the back of a spoon. You should see some froth or bubbles form on the surface of the liquid. The ferment will develop the lightly sour smell typical of lacto-fermentation, but because these are chile peppers, the aroma will also have a spicy kick.

6. Let the peppers actively ferment at room temperature for at least a few days before moving them to the refrigerator or a cool cellar. They won't need the plate under them anymore once they are in cold storage. The flavor of the hot sauce will continue to develop over time, and it will keep, chilled, for at least a year.

FERMENTING FRUIT

Fruits host just as many Lactobacillus bacteria as vegetables do and therefore are just as easy to ferment. Although we tend to value most fruits for their sweetness, lacto-fermented fruits have a blend of sweet and sour that pairs wonderfully with savory foods, including main-course meats and rich cheeses.

Fermented Apple Salsa

PREP TIME: 15 minutes   INITIAL FERMENTATION TIME: 2 days   YIELD: 1 quart

---

This is my variation on nutritionist Sally Fallon's lacto-fermented apple chutney. If you start with firm, recently harvested apples, the result is a crisp fruit salsa that combines sweet, sour, and salty flavors. It makes a great accompaniment for roasted meat or poultry, as well as curries, but is also excellent served as a side salad on top of cucumbers (you won't need any dressing besides the apple salsa).

INGREDIENTS

½ cup filtered or non-chlorinated water

2 tablespoons honey

2 tablespoons whey (optional but useful; see the sidebar elsewhere in this chapter for how to make whey)

1 tablespoon apple cider vinegar

2 teaspoons kosher or medium-grain sea salt

1 teaspoon coriander seeds

½ teaspoon caraway seeds

½ cup raisins

¼ cup thinly sliced onion

1 teaspoon ground cumin

½–1 teaspoon red pepper flakes

½ teaspoon dried thyme

1. Whisk the water, honey, whey, apple cider vinegar, and salt until the honey and salt are completely dissolved.

2. Peel and core the apples. Chop them into pieces or slivers between ⅛ and ¼ inch thick.

3. Lightly grind the coriander and caraway seeds with a mortar and pestle.

4. Coarsely chop the raisins (you can skip this step if you like, but I think the texture of the salsa is better if you take the time).

5. In a large bowl, mix together the apples, raisins, onion slices, and all of the spices. Pack the combined ingredients into a clean glass quart jar.

6. Pour the brine over the other ingredients. The brine should completely cover the solid ingredients; if it doesn't, top off with a little filtered water.

7. Put a lid on the jar, but loosely (you want the gases that develop during fermentation to be able to escape). Put a small plate under the jar to catch any overflow that may occur during fermentation.

8. Leave the jar of apple salsa out at room temperature for 2 days. During that time, take the lid off at least once a day and look for signs of fermentation such as bubbles on the surface. You'll see these especially if you press gently on the food. But don't just look for signs of fermentation; also get close with your nose and sniff for that clean but tangy pickled smell that means the safe, tasty, and healthy transformation you're after is happening. Because of the spices, your fermenting fruit salsa will be more aromatic than plain vegetable ferments are.

9. Once the apple salsa has been actively fermenting for at least 24 hours, transfer it to the refrigerator or a cool, dark cellar. You won't need the plate under the jar any longer, because the cold storage temperature will slow down fermentation so much that there shouldn't be any overflow. If you opt for the refrigerator, store the apple salsa on the top shelf of the main compartment where it is coolest. This will help the apples keep their crunch longer. Wait at least a week longer before eating the salsa.

CHAPTER TWO

Boiling Water Bath Canning

Say "food preservation" to many people and the first thing they think of is canning. That's interesting because canning is actually a relatively new method of preserving food (less than 200 years old, compared with techniques such as lacto-fermentation that have been used for thousands of years).

The word *canning* itself is somewhat confusing. Unlike commercial canned foods, very little home canning is done in metal cans anymore. Instead, glass canning jars with specially designed lids are the go-to equipment. I've heard people use the term *jarring* instead of canning, which is more accurate. But jarring also means "shocking" or "jolting"—so I'm going to stick with the old-fashioned term.

There are two methods of canning: In a boiling water bath and in a pressure canner. Knowing the difference between the two methods is absolutely essential if you want to preserve food safely in sealed jars that will be stored at room temperature.

Boiling water bath canning is the simpler of the two methods. It requires minimal equipment—basically just a large, deep pot plus canning jars and lids. The most important thing to know about canning in a boiling water bath is that this method is *only safe with high-acid foods.*

What are high-acid foods? Fruits, anything pickled with a vinegar-based brine (including chutneys); fruit-based sweet preserves such as jams and jellies; and tomatoes with a little added acidity (more about that later). To be safely preserved in a boiling water bath, the food in the jars needs to have a pH of 4.6 or lower. See the appendix for a chart of the pH values of different foods.

Jars filled with any of those foods can be safely processed in a boiling water bath. *All other foods including nonpickled vegetables, soup stocks, and meats must be processed in a pressure canner.* Pressure canning is such a different process that it gets its own chapter.

The heat processing in the boiling water bath does contribute to the safe preservation of the food, but does not by itself guarantee the contents will be safe to eat. The takeaway here is that with a boiling water bath, it is the acidity of each jar's contents—even more than the heat of the processing—that safely preserves the food.

In conjunction with canning jars and lids, the boiling water bath creates a vacuum seal that prevents molds from entering the jars. But as with store-bought canned foods, once the jars are opened they must be stored in the refrigerator.

You may come across old-fashioned suggestions to seal your canning jars by turning them upside down while the food in the jars is still hot, or by placing them in the oven. Don't do it! Although the jars may seal, a true vacuum may not have been created. Also, with those methods the food inside may not have reached the temperature of boiling water all the way through to its very center.

Canning times (also called processing times) are based on the density of the food and the size of the jar, both of which affect how long it takes for all the food to reach the temperature of the surrounding hot water.

> ### EQUIPMENT FOR A BOILING WATER BATH
>
> - A tall pot such as a stock- or pasta pot
> - A rack or dishtowel to place in the bottom of the pot
> - Canning jars and lids
> - A timer or clock
> - A jar lifter (optional, but recommended)

How to Process Jars of Food in a Boiling Water Bath

SET UP THE CANNING EQUIPMENT

Place a rack or a dish towel in the bottom of the pot. This is to prevent the glass jars from cracking when they get bounced around by the boiling water. A round cake rack works well. If you have a pressure canner, you can "borrow" the round rack that came with it. If you don't have a suitable rack, you can use a dish towel. Make sure the towel is weighted down by enough jars to cover it. If you are only canning one or two jars of food, fill the canner with extra "dummy" jars that are filled with plain water. This will prevent the dish towel from floating and tipping over the jars of food.

Place the pot on the stove. Add enough water so that it will cover the closed lids of the jars by 1 to 2 inches. Again, that's 1 to 2 inches *above* the lids of the jars. This is important because you need the food to heat evenly from all directions, not just from the bottom. Turn the heat up to high.

If you need to sterilize the jars (see the sidebar in this chapter) for the recipe you are making, you can do so directly in the boiling water bath. If not, wash the jars and keep them filled with hot water until you are ready to fill them with the food (filling cold jars with hot food could cause the jars to crack).

LOAD THE JARS

Pour out the hot water in the jars, then fill them according to the recipe you are using. Leave at least ½ inch head space between the top of the food and the tops of the jars. Wipe the rims with a lightly moistened, clean paper or cloth towel (any bits of food there could prevent a seal).

Most boiling water bath recipes should be hot packed, meaning that the ingredients should be piping hot when they go into the jars. If you're pressed for time, you can cook the ingredients, refrigerate them overnight, and then reheat them the next day before filling the jars and canning them.

Screw on the canning lids. Lower the jars into the pot on top of the rack or dishtowel. Try to set them up so that there is ½ inch of space between the sides of the jars. If the water doesn't cover the jars by 1 to 2 inches, add more hot water.

DON'T DO THIS!

There is quite a bit of erroneous information out there about canning and sterilizing canning equipment. A lot of it comes from previous generations when people assumed that this new canning process must be similar to the fermenting and other forms of food preservation that they'd used previously. Remember that canning equipment and methods like those we use today were not invented until the 19th century, and modern canning lids not until the 20th century.

With apologies to my parents' generation, an additional source of potentially dangerous canning advice comes from the abundance of semi-accurate food preservation information from the 1960s and '70s back-to-the-land movement. "Semi-accurate" is not accurate enough when it comes to food safety.

Here are some of the most common, potentially dangerous "techniques" still being advocated. I see these frequently on DIY blogs and recipe collection websites. Please do not use any of these methods—why risk it? The safe ways to preserve food explained in this book are just as easy.

- *Do not* use your oven or your dishwasher to "sterilize" canning jars.
- *Do not* skip boiling water bath or pressure canner processing for canning foods and instead turn jars upside down for a few minutes before setting them upright.
- *Do not* pour melted paraffin wax over hot food and consider it sealed. First of all, paraffin is a petroleum product, and not only are we trying to reduce our dependence on petroleum products but there are lots of health alerts about having them in direct contact with our food. Second, any bubble or air tunnel in the wax could create an imperfect seal, resulting in mold or food that doesn't keep as long as expected.

PROCESS THE JARS IN THE BOILING WATER BATH

Wait until the water comes to a full, vigorous boil. When it does, start timing the processing according to the recipe instructions.

COOLING DOWN

When the processing time is up, remove the jars from the boiling water bath (this is where a jar lifter comes in handy, but you can use tongs). Place the jars somewhere that they can cool down undisturbed for at least 6 hours. If you are going to set them on a cold countertop, first lay down a towel so that the piping-hot glass jars don't crack on contact with the cold surface.

The reason for the long undisturbed cooling-down phase is that during this time a vacuum seal forms. Jostling a jar might bring the hot contents in contact with the underside of the lid. That could prevent a seal, or undo one that has just formed. Leave the jars alone until they've cooled completely, or be *very* careful not to jostle the contents if you must move them while they are still warm.

CHECK THE SEALS

Once the jars have cooled, the lids should be slightly concave and feel solid when you press down on their centers. Unsealed lids will still be flexible and spring back up after you press on them.

You can further test the seals of two-piece canning lids by removing the outer ring (which is only there to hold the inner lid on during the processing). Lift the jar, holding it only by the edges of the inner lid. If it's sealed, that inner lid will remain securely fastened. It is fine to store sealed jars without the outer screwbands.

If any of your jars have not sealed, you have a choice: You can either put on new lids and reprocess the jars in a boiling water bath for the original amount of time specified in the recipe, or keep the unsealed jars in the refrigerator and eat the contents within a week.

Stovetop Applesauce

PREP TIME: 10 minutes   COOKING TIME: 25 minutes   BOILING WATER BATH TIME: 20 minutes
YIELD: 4–5 pints

Applesauce is a much more versatile ingredient than many people realize. Sure, it's a healthy snack to include in your kid's lunchbox, and a classic side dish to go with pork. But you can also use it to replace some of the fat in sweet baked goods, and even take it in a savory direction by combining it with winter squash in pureed soups.

You can also make this sauce with pears, plums, peaches, and apricots.

INGREDIENTS

3 pounds apples
2 tablespoons sugar *or* 1½ tablespoons honey (optional)
½ cup water or apple juice
2 tablespoons lemon juice

1. Wash the apples. If you have a food mill or a food processor, you'll use it later to deal with the peels. Otherwise, peel the apples. Remove the cores (save them to make Apple Scrap Vinegar; the recipe is in the Vinegar Pickling chapter). Chop the apples into chunks about an inch thick.

2. Put the apples into a large pot. If you are using the sugar, add it to the apples; if you are using the honey, dissolve it in the water. Add the lemon juice and the water to the pot.

3. Cook the apples over medium heat, stirring frequently, for 20 to 25 minutes until they are mushy. If you left the peels on, run the applesauce through a food mill to remove them, or puree in a food processor (peels and all). If you peeled the apples, you can either mash them with a potato masher or puree them in a blender or food processor. Homemade applesauce will keep, refrigerated, for 1 week, or in the freezer for 6 months.

4. For longer storage at room temperature, fill clean, hot pint or half-pint jars with the applesauce, leaving ½ inch of head space. The applesauce should still be hot when you fill the jars. If you want to can applesauce that has already cooled or been in the refrigerator for a couple of days, first bring it to a boil over medium heat before filling the jars.

5. Go around the insides of the filled jars with a table knife to remove any air bubbles. Wipe the rims of the jars clean. Screw on canning lids and process in a boiling water bath for 20 minutes (adjust the canning time for your altitude if necessary; see the sidebar in this chapter).

BOILING WATER BATH CANNING
AT HIGH ALTITUDES

I've explained that boiling water bath canning relies on a combination of the acidity of the ingredients and the heat of the boiling water to safely preserve food. But water boils at different temperatures depending on altitude, because the higher the altitude, the lower the atmospheric pressure.

The majority of people on this planet live at 1,000 feet above sea level or lower. At those altitudes, water boils at 212°F, and canning recipes generally assume that you are at an altitude where that is the temperature of your boiling water bath. But at 2,500 feet, water boils at just 207.1°F. Because of this difference, if you live more that 1,000 feet above sea level, you need to adjust the canning times given in boiling water bath recipes. Pressure canning at high altitudes is a different adjustment that I explain in that chapter.

Here are the adjustments for boiling water bath processing at high altitudes.

BOILING WATER BATH PROCESSING ALTITUDE ADJUSTMENT		
ALTITUDE	PROCESSING TIME LESS THAN 20 MINUTES	PROCESSING TIME MORE THAN 20 MINUTES
1,001–3,000 feet	increase time by 5 minutes	increase time by 5 minutes
3,001–6,000 feet	increase time by 10 minutes	
6,001+ feet	increase time by 15 minutes	increase time by 10 minutes

For example, if the recipe calls for processing jars of tomatoes in a boiling water bath for 35 minutes and you live at 5,000 feet above sea level, you'll need to process them for 45 minutes instead.

How to Can Tomatoes

Tomatoes are one of the first foods many people try to can, partly because canning them is relatively easy. However, gone are the days when you could simply smash some raw tomatoes into a canning jar, process them in a boiling water bath for a while, and call it done. To can modern tomato varieties safely in a boiling water bath (rather than a pressure canner), you need to add some acidity. Here's why.

Over the past several decades, many varieties of tomato have been bred for sweetness. Whereas old-fashioned tomatoes had enough natural acidity that you could safely can them without any other ingredients, many of today's tomato varieties require added acid to bring their pH low enough for boiling water bath canning. If you do not do this, you will need to process your tomatoes in a pressure canner rather than a boiling water bath (something I do not recommend, because the flavor is not as good).

Per pint jar of tomatoes, add 1 tablespoon of lemon juice or vinegar, or ¼ teaspoon of citric acid. For quart jars, double those amounts. I don't really notice a difference in the taste, but if you're worried that it might be too sour, you can add a little sugar to offset the added acidity. If you opt for lemon juice, it's best to use bottled. I know, I know—fresh citrus juice always tastes better, and that is what I use for regular cooking. But in this case it's not about flavor, it's about food safety, and bottled lemon juice has a consistent level of acidity that fresh lemons don't always have.

You may come across old-time instructions for canning pasta sauces and other tomato-based products that say they may be safely canned in a boiling bath because of the acidity of the tomatoes. Again, this is no longer considered safe. For example, plain zucchini is a low-acid vegetable that must be pressure canned. Adding tomato sauce to zucchini does not increase its acidity enough to make it safe for boiling water bath canning (and if you did add enough acidity from lemon juice, vinegar, or the like, it would taste more like a pickle than a vegetable). You may, however, pressure can such combinations of unpickled vegetables.

Four Ways to Can Tomatoes

RAW PACK

The raw pack method involves simply smashing chopped-up raw tomatoes (and added acid, as described above) into clean jars, then processing in a boiling water bath. It is certainly the easiest way to can tomatoes, but it is also my least favorite.

The disadvantages of the raw pack method are longer processing times and a watery product that tends to separate once it cools in the jars (the red pulp floats unattractively above a layer of almost clear, yellowish liquid).

But if you really need to get the tomato canning project done in a hurry, raw pack is better than not canning any tomatoes at all. Despite the longer processing time, it is still slightly quicker than the other methods.

Be sure to leave at least ½-inch head space between the surface of the food and the rims of the jars. Wipe the jar rims clean before screwing the lids on. Process pint jars of tomatoes in a boiling water bath for 40 minutes, quarts for 45 minutes. Adjust the canning time if you live at a high altitude (see the sidebar in this chapter).

HOT PACK

The hot pack method is almost as easy as the raw pack, but results in a less watery product that doesn't separate as much.

Remove the whitish stem ends and cores of the tomatoes and compost or discard them. Chop the tomatoes and put them into a large pot. Bring them to a boil over medium-high heat, stirring. Boil the tomatoes for 5 minutes.

Fill clean canning jars with the hot tomatoes, adding acid in the amounts described above, and leaving ½ inch of head space in each jar. Screw on the canning lids. Process in a boiling water bath, 30 minutes for pints, 35 minutes for quarts. Adjust the canning time if you live at a high altitude (see the sidebar in this chapter).

A BETTER HOT PACK: BLANCHED AND PEELED

This method requires a couple of extra steps, but if you have the time the result is much more colorful and flavorful.

Place a large pot of water over high heat. Cut out the stem ends of the tomatoes and compost or discard them. Once the water is at a full boil, drop in the tomatoes. After about 30 seconds, the skins will split and start to curl in a few places. Lift the tomatoes out of the hot water with a slotted spoon and let them drain in a colander.

The skins have been loosened by their brief blanching and should be easy to rub or peel off (but don't worry if you don't get every single bit). Squish out the tomato seed gel and either discard it or use it to make tomato water.

Pack the peeled, seeded tomatoes into clean pint canning jars, pressing down with your clean fingers or the back of a spoon to remove any air bubbles. As you put in the tomatoes, add 1 tablespoon of vinegar or bottled lemon juice to each jar, or ¼ teaspoon citric acid. Press the tomatoes with your clean fingers or the back of a spoon to remove any air bubbles. Leave ½ inch head space in each jar. Screw on canning lids. Process pints for 30 minutes, quarts for 35 minutes. Adjust the canning time if you live at a high altitude (see the sidebar in this chapter).

SOMETHING SPECIAL: ROASTED TOMATOES

This is hands-down my favorite method for canning tomatoes. Instead of blanching them in water, core the tomatoes and arrange them in a single layer on a baking sheet. Preheat your oven's broiler. Broil the tomatoes until the skins start to blacken in a few spots (but don't let them burn all over). This roasting accomplishes the same loosening of the skins that the water blanching does, but also wonderfully intensifies the flavor of the tomatoes.

Once the tomatoes are roasted, proceed with the hot pack blanched-and-peeled tomato canning instructions.

How to Can Peaches and Other Fruit (With or Without Sugar)

I'm using peaches in these instructions because they are the quintessential canning fruit. Not only do home-canned peaches look beautiful in the jars, but you can use them in everything from fruit salad to quick breads. But the canning method here applies to other fruits as well.

There are two ways to safely can peaches and other fruit: hot pack or raw pack. I am not a fan of the raw pack method because it almost always results in fruit float, which is when the fruit floats up out of the liquid it is canned in. Raw pack fruit that floats to the top turns an unappealing brownish color. There's much less likelihood of that happening with the hot pack method.

1. Examine the peaches and choose those that have no bruises or other blemishes for canning (use imperfect fruit for chopped recipes such as chutney). The peaches will have better flavor if ripe, but better texture once canned if underripe: Split the difference and choose peaches that are aromatic but still firm. If you intend to can peach halves rather than chunks or slices, be sure to choose a freestone rather than a clingstone variety of peach (clingstone peaches are nearly impossible to separate from the pits in neat halves).

2. Set up your boiling water bath.

3. Bring a large pot of water (separate from your boiling water bath) to a boil over high heat. If you're

canning freestone peach halves, cut then twist the peaches in half and discard the pits. If you're working with clingstone peaches, cut a small x in one end of each peach. Drop the peaches into the boiling water for 10 seconds. This step makes it easier to peel the peaches, but also prevents discoloration in the peeled fruit.

4. Drain the blanched peaches in a colander, and when they are cool enough to handle, peel them. You can also scrape off the darker areas where the pits were with a spoon, but this is optional.

5. If desired, cut the peaches into slices or chunks. If you are working with clingstone peaches, it's easiest to cut the pieces right off the pits rather than trying to first remove the pits.

6. Until recently, peaches have usually been canned in a simple sugar syrup made of equal parts sugar and water, or sometimes twice as much sugar as water. Although it is certainly still possible to do that, in these more health-conscious times it makes better sense to can peaches and other fruit in unsweetened juice. You could also use plain water, but I find that some of the flavor of the fruit leaches out into the water, resulting in a bland final product. My favorite juice to use for canning fruit is white grape juice because of its relatively neutral flavor and color.

    Bring the canning liquid of your choice (sugar syrup, juice, or water) to a boil. Add the peeled and sliced peaches and simmer them for 2 minutes.

7. Transfer the peaches to clean, hot canning jars using a slotted spoon. Pack in the fruit tightly, but leave ¾-inch head space between the surface of the fruit and the rims of the jars. Pour the hot liquid the peaches simmered in over the fruit. The peaches should be completely covered by the liquid, and there should still be ½ inch of head space. Press down on the fruit gently with the back of a spoon to release any air bubbles.

8. Wipe the rims of the jars clean and screw on the canning lids. Process the jars of peaches in a boiling water bath, 20 minutes for pints or 25 minutes for quarts. Adjust the canning time for your altitude if necessary.

How to Can Blueberries and Other Berries with No Other Ingredients

This beautifully simple technique contains only one ingredient: blueberries. The result keeps all the flavor of the fresh fruit, although with a softer texture. You can also use this method with juneberries, blackberries, raspberries, wineberries, currants, and gooseberries.

1. Bring a pot of water to a boil. While you are waiting for the water to boil, sort through the blueberries and discard any that are shriveled or not fully ripe. Wash the fruit and let it drain in a colander for a minute or two.

2. Work with about a pint of blueberries at a time. Tie the blueberries up into a loose bundle in a single layer of cheesecloth. The cheesecloth should be securely tied, but the blueberries should not be packed together too tightly—you want water to be able to circulate among them.

3. Hold on to the knot end of the cheesecloth bundle with a pair of tongs. Dip the blueberries into the pot of boiling water and gently swirl the bundle in the water. Keep doing this for 30 seconds. By the end of the 30 seconds you should see a few juice stains appear on the cheesecloth.

4. Untie the cheesecloth (it's fine to reuse it for the next pint of blueberries). Transfer the blueberries to a clean canning jar, loosely filling the jar with the blanched fruit. Leave ½-inch head space. This method is unusual in that you do not add any liquid, not even water. Screw on the canning lid. Repeat the blanching and jar-filling steps with the remainder of your blueberries.

5. Process pint jars of blanched blueberries in a boiling water bath for 15 minutes, quarts for 20. Adjust those processing times for your altitude if necessary.

> **NOTE**
>
> See the chapters on Vinegar Pickling and on Sweet Preserves for more boiling water bath recipes.

CHAPTER THREE

Vinegar Pickling

Pickles that are preserved by the acidity of vinegar range in flavor from sharply sour cornichons to spicy chutney to sweet red pepper relish, and in texture from crisp dill refrigerator cucumbers to smooth sauces such as ketchup (yes, ketchup is technically a vinegar pickle).

There is another food preservation technique also often called pickling, and that is lacto-fermentation (which has its own chapter in this book). Some folks say you should *only* refer to fermented foods as pickled, but there are also those who insist that it's only the vinegar-based ones that deserve to be called pickles. The most important thing to know is that in both kinds of pickling, it is the pH of the brine that ultimately preserves the food.

There are three kinds of vinegar pickling:

- Refrigerator pickles, because of the cool temperatures they are stored at, require very little vinegar to be safely preserved; they have a milder flavor and usually more crunch than canned vinegar pickles. The safety factor here is a combination of some acidity in the brine plus cold storage.

- Canned vinegar pickles have a more pungent, in-your-nose acidity that is a plus for recipes such as cornichons and spiced pickled carrots, but usually too tart for a go-with-your-sandwich-style pickle.

  With canned vinegar pickles, it is the acidity of the ingredients even more than the heat and seal of the boiling water bath canning that safely preserves the food. The ingredients must have a pH of 4.6 or less to be preserved with this method. You can buy pH meters that will tell you how acidic your recipe is, or you can follow this rule: Never dilute the vinegar in your brine with more than an equal amount of water (this assumes that you are starting with a vinegar that contains 4.5 percent or higher acetic acid, as almost all commercial vinegars do—it will say on the label). If pickles made with 50–50 vinegar and water are still too sour for you, try one of the other two kinds of vinegar pickling, or opt for lacto-fermented pickles instead.

- The third type of vinegar pickle is the kind that has enough vinegar acidity for safe boiling water bath canning, but buffers the flavor with sweet- ness from sugar or honey. Sweet-and-sour pickle recipes include bread-and-butter pickles, hot-dog-style relishes, chutneys, and ketchups. Usually there is no water added to these types of recipes.

In terms of flavor, apple cider vinegar, as well as red and white wine vinegars, are all excellent for pickling. White distilled vinegar has the advantage of showing off the bright colors of some vegetables such as chile peppers or carrots, but can have a slightly astringent aftertaste.

Quick Refrigerator Dill Pickles

PREP TIME: 15 minutes   YIELD: 1 quart

The difference between fabulous and so-so cucumber pickles is choosing small, firm cucumbers with hardly any seeds. It's not essential to use a pickling variety of cucumber, but use only those that are not more than an inch in diameter and feel solid.

INGREDIENTS

2 pounds small, firm cucumbers

1 pint water

¼ cup plus 2 tablespoons cider or white wine vinegar

1½ tablespoons kosher or other non-iodized salt

1 tablespoon sugar or 2 teaspoons light honey (clover or wildflower works well)

2–4 cloves garlic

1 teaspoon whole mustard seeds

½ teaspoon whole black peppercorns

2–4 small grape leaves or 3-inch pieces of horseradish leaf (optional)

2–3 dill flowerheads or 2 generous sprigs fresh dill leaves or 1 tablespoon dried dillweed

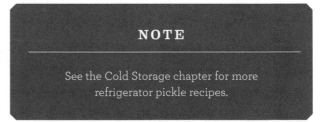

NOTE

See the Cold Storage chapter for more refrigerator pickle recipes.

HOW TO MAKE REFRIGERATOR PICKLES

Although I'm using cucumbers in this recipe, you can also use carrots, cauliflower, radishes, or pretty much any vegetable to make these refrigerator pickles. They have a light, deli dill flavor and good crunch, and are ready to eat just a few days after you make them. In theory, these pickles will keep, refrigerated, for at least three months, but mine always get eaten up well before then. Note that there is not enough vinegar in this recipe to safely can them for storage at room temperature. These must be refrigerated. It is the combination of acidity and cold storage that safely preserves them.

INSTRUCTIONS

1. Cut a thin sliver off the flower end of the cucumbers (that's opposite the stem end, but if you're not sure, slice off both ends.) The end of the cucumber that once had the flower attached contains enzymes that can soften pickles, so slicing off that little bit can result in better, crunchier pickles.

2. Slice the cucumbers lengthwise into halves or spears, or leave very small cucumbers whole.

3. Bring the water, vinegar, salt, and sugar or honey to a boil, stirring occasionally. Once the brine reaches a boil, turn off the heat and let it cool to room temperature (it's fine to speed this up by putting the brine into the refrigerator.)

4. Put the garlic, mustard seeds, peppercorns, and one of the grape or horseradish leavs (if using) into the bottom of a clean glass jar. Because these pickles are destined for the refrigerator, not the canner, you do not need to use canning jars.

5. Tip the jar onto its side and start packing in the cucumbers. Once there are enough cucumbers in the jar to keep them lined up straight, set the jar upright to finish loading the ingredients. You want the cucumbers to be packed in so tightly that they hold one another in place under the brine—keep adding until you can't get one more in. Tuck in the dill and remaining leaves as you add the cucumbers.

6. Pour the cooled brine over the cucumbers. They should be completely covered by the liquid. Screw on the lid, and put your pickles-to-be in the refrigerator.

7. Wait 4 to 5 days for the flavor of the pickles to develop before tasting them.

Pickled Whole Chile Peppers

PREP TIME: 5 minutes   CANNING TIME: 10 minutes   YIELD: 1 pint

This may be the easiest vinegar pickle recipe ever. If, like me, you love spicy food, you'll want to put up several jars of pickled chile peppers. I use them anytime a recipe calls for a jalapeño or other pepper. They also make a colorful gift. When you've eaten all the peppers, use the spicy vinegar that's left as hot sauce.

INGREDIENTS

1 pint chile peppers, any kind
1½ cups white wine or distilled vinegar

TIP

If you grow your own chile peppers, get a jar of these started in the refrigerator and add a few peppers at a time as you have them. Top off with vinegar as needed.

INSTRUCTIONS

1. Slice off the stem ends of the peppers. Leave small peppers whole, but remove the seeds from larger chile peppers and cut them into strips. You could also cut the peppers crosswise into rings.

2. If you are going to store the pickled peppers in the refrigerator, you can put them into any clean glass jar. For storage at room temperature, use a canning jar and lid. Pack the prepped peppers into the jar, leaving an inch of head space.

3. Pour the vinegar over the peppers. If they are going into the fridge, simply secure the lid and you're done. Otherwise, make sure the peppers are completely immersed in the vinegar and that there is still ½-inch head space. Screw on the canning lid and process in a boiling water bath for 10 minutes.

Cornichon Pickles

PREP TIME: 5 minutes   SALTING TIME: 24 hours
YIELD: Makes, well, it depends on how many baby cukes you have

---

These are the piquant, pinkie-finger-sized cucumber pickles served in France alongside pâté and cheese appetizers. Their sharp flavor perfectly offsets the richness of the other foods they are served with. They are incredibly easy to make, with one caveat: You will need to either grow your own cucumbers or make friends with someone who does. The cucumbers should be less than 3 inches long and 1/2 inch thick, which is a size nearly impossible to find at the market. One of the terrific things about making cornichons is that you needn't have all the baby cucumbers at once in order to proceed: You can add them a few at a time as they come in from the garden.

Making cornichons uses a combination of salting and vinegar pickling food preservation techniques.

INGREDIENTS

Baby cucumbers about the size of your little finger

Kosher or other non-iodized salt

Pearl onions (optional)

Bay leaf (optional)

Black peppercorns (optional)

White wine vinegar

INSTRUCTIONS

1. Wash the cucumbers. Slice a thin sliver off the blossom end (if you aren't sure which end that is, cut a sliver off both ends).

2. Spread a layer of salt in a bowl and place the baby cucumbers on top. Bury the cucumbers in more salt. Repeat with alternating layers of baby cucumbers and salt. Leave in the refrigerator or cool cellar for 24 hours.

3. Brush the salt off the cucumbers. Put them in a jar along with the optional pearl onions and spices, and cover them with the vinegar. Store in the refrigerator. Salt and add more baby cucumbers as you have them, always adding vinegar to cover.

NOTE

Cornichons will keep, refrigerated or in other cold storage (see that chapter), for at least 6 months. For longer storage at room temperature, process them in sterilized jars in a boiling water bath for 5 minutes (adjust the canning time if you live at a high altitude; see the sidebar in the Boiling Water Bath Canning chapter).

Bread-and-Butter Pickles

PREP TIME: 10 minutes   COOKING TIME: 10 minutes   SALTING TIME: 4 hours
CANNING TIME: 5 minutes   YIELD: 5–6 half-pint jars

Bread-and-butter pickles are flavored and preserved by a sweet-and-sour brine. Although sugar or honey is added for flavoring, it is primarily the acidity of the vinegar that preserves them.

These sliced pickles are delicious in their namesake sandwich, which is nothing more than bread, butter, and pickles. But they are also terrific on their own, or added to other sandwiches.

INGREDIENTS

2½ pounds firm, small cucumbers

¾ pound onions, peeled and sliced thinly

1 large red bell pepper, stemmed, seeded, and finely chopped

3 tablespoons kosher or other non-iodized salt

1½ cups apple cider vinegar

1½ cups sugar or 1 cup honey

¾ cup water

1 tablespoon mustard seeds

1 teaspoon whole allspice

1 teaspoon celery seeds

INSTRUCTIONS

1. While the jars are sterilizing, slice the cucumbers into thin rounds. Toss the cucumber slices with the onions, bell pepper, and salt. Put the salted vegetables into a colander set in a large bowl. Let the vegetables drain for 4 hours.

2. If you plan to store the pickles in sealed jars at room temperature rather than refrigerating them right away, sterilize the canning jars.

3. Rinse the vegetables under cool water to remove most of the salt. Transfer them to a large pot and add the rest of the ingredients.

4. Bring the ingredients to a boil over high heat, stirring to dissolve the sugar or honey. Turn off the heat as soon as the liquid comes to a boil.

5. With a slotted spoon, transfer the vegetables to the sterilized jars (or simply clean glass jars if you plan to refrigerate rather than can the pickles). Pack them in fairly tightly, but leave an inch of head space.

6. Pour the hot brine over the vegetables. You want the pickles to be completely covered by the brine, but still have ½ inch of head space. Lightly press down on the pickles with the back of a spoon to release any air bubbles.

7. Screw on the lids and refrigerate immediately. Or screw on the canning lids and process in a boiling water bath for 5 minutes (adjust the canning time if you live at a high altitude; see the sidebar in the Boiling Water Bath Canning chapter).

8. Wait 4 days before eating the pickles. They will taste even better after a week.

Dilly Beans

PREP TIME: 5 minutes   CANNING TIME: 10 minutes
YIELD: 1 pint; recipe can be multiplied

This is *the* classic way to pickle green beans. I eat them as is, but you can also chop them up and add them to salads including mayonnaise-based ones such as egg salad. For a colorful version that looks lovely in the jar and on your plate, use a combination of green beans and yellow wax beans.

INGREDIENTS

¾ pound green beans and/or yellow wax beans

1–2 cloves garlic, smashed

4–6 whole black peppercorns

½ teaspoon whole mustard seeds

2–3 fresh sprigs dill leaves, or fresh dill flower heads

1 cup white wine vinegar

½ cup water

1 teaspoon kosher or other non-iodized salt

1 teaspoon honey

1. Wash the beans, remove the stem ends, and trim them so that they will fit into a pint-sized canning jar lengthwise with an inch of head space above them.

2. Put the garlic, pepper, and mustard seeds into a clean, pint-sized canning jar. Tip the jar onto its side. Load in the green and/or wax beans. When the jar is full enough for the beans to stay vertical, set it upright.

3. Tuck in the dill sprigs or flower heads. A chopstick is useful for pushing the herbs down into the beans.

4. Add more beans until they are so tightly packed that you can't shove in a single bean more without it breaking. The beans will shrink slightly during canning, and you want them to be so tightly packed that even with that shrinkage they hold one another down under the vinegar brine.

5. Put the vinegar, water, salt, and honey into a small pot and bring them to a boil over high heat, stirring to dissolve the honey.

6. Pour the hot vinegar brine over the beans and other ingredients in the jar. Be sure that the food is completely immersed in the brine, but there is still 1/2 inch of head space.

7. Wipe the rim of the jar clean. Screw on the canning lid. Process in a boiling water bath for 10 minutes. Adjust the canning time if you live at a high altitude (see the Boiling Water Bath Canning chapter).

8. Wait 1 to 2 weeks for the flavors to develop before serving.

Naturally Pink Cauliflower Pickles

PREP TIME: 10 minutes   COOKING TIME: 1 minute   CANNING TIME: 10 minutes

YIELD: 2 pints

This recipe is my version of a treat I have enjoyed when traveling in the Middle East, where a variety of pickles are usually served alongside hummus and other small dishes. The bright pink color comes from including a few slices of beet root along with the cauliflower. If instead of cauliflower you are using an already colorful ingredient such as carrots, simply leave out the beet but keep the vinegar-to-water ratio of the brine the same.

INGREDIENTS

1 medium-small cauliflower (1½–2 pounds)

1 small beet

2 sprigs fresh dill or 2 dill flower heads or 1 teaspoon dried dillweed, divided

2 small cloves garlic, peeled and lightly smashed

1 teaspoon mustard seeds, divided

½ teaspoon cumin seeds, divided

½ teaspoon red chile pepper flakes, divided (optional)

1 cup white distilled or white wine vinegar

¾ cup water

1 tablespoon honey

2 teaspoons kosher or other non-iodized salt

INSTRUCTIONS

1. Wash the cauliflower and remove any outer leaves. Cut it in half, and slice off the florets with a short length of the base attached. Aim for approximately 1-inch pieces.

2. Peel the beet. Cut it in half and then into ½-inch-thick slices.

3. Distribute the dill, garlic cloves, and spices between two clean pint canning jars. Pack in the cauliflower above the seasonings, adding half of the beet slices to each jar. Leave 1 inch of head space.

4. Combine the vinegar, water, honey, and salt in a small pot. Bring to a boil, stirring to dissolve the salt and honey. Skim off any foam that forms on the surface. Pour the hot brine over the other ingredients in the jars, fully covering them but still leaving ½ inch of head space.

5. Screw on canning lids and process the jars in a boiling water bath for 10 minutes (adjust the canning time if you live at a high altitude—see the sidebar in the Boiling Water Bath Canning chapter). Wait at least one week before serving. During that time, not only will the flavors mellow and "marry," but the beet juices will color the cauliflower.

Green Tomato Chutney

PREP TIME: 10 minutes   COOKING TIME: 20 minutes   CANNING TIME: 10 minutes
YIELD: 3 pints

You can make this chutney master recipe with other ingredients (try swapping pears or peaches for the tomatoes), but I think it is special when made with green tomatoes at the end of the gardening season.

INGREDIENTS

6 cups finely chopped green tomatoes

1 large, tart apple, peeled, cored, and finely chopped

2 cups light brown sugar or 1 1/2 cups honey

2 cups apple cider vinegar

1½ cups raisins, chopped

1 organic lemon, sliced into thin slivers (include the peels but discard the seeds)

¼ cup peeled and minced fresh gingerroot

1 clove garlic, peeled and minced

1–2 chile peppers, minced

½ teaspoon salt

¼ teaspoon ground allspice

¼ teaspoon ground coriander seeds

Pinch of ground cloves

NOTE

Chutney is a versatile condiment with many uses besides playing sidekick to curried dishes.

INSTRUCTIONS

1. Put all of the ingredients in a large pot over medium-high heat.

2. Boil, stirring often, until the green tomatoes and the apple are very soft. The chutney is thick enough when a wooden spoon dragged across the pot bottom leaves a trail that doesn't fill in with chutney until a couple of seconds have passed.

3. Green tomato chutney will keep in the refrigerator for up to 1 month. For longer storage at room temperature, can the chutney in pint or half-pint jars in a boiling water bath for 10 minutes (adjust the canning time if you live at a high altitude; see the sidebar in the Boiling Water Bath Canning chapter)

TEN WAYS TO USE CHUTNEY

1. The classic curry condiment: Spoon some chutney straight out of the jar and serve it alongside any East Indian–style curry recipe.

2. Easy party spread or dip: Chutney plus cream cheese or labneh (yogurt cheese; see the Dairy chapter) is an appetizing combination. There are a few different ways to serve it. The easiest is simply to put some cream cheese or labneh on a plate and spoon any variety of chutney over it. Surround the chutney-covered cheese with crackers and make sure there is a small spreading knife for your guests to use.

    The other way is to puree a little chutney together with the cheese in a food processor (or you could mash it up with a fork). Add a small splash of milk for a thinner consistency if you want more of a dip than a spread.

3. Cheater's ketchup: Compare the ingredients of a chutney with those of a ketchup and you will notice that they have an identical blend of sweet (usually sugar) and sour (almost always vinegar), combined with a fruit or vegetable and spices. The takeaway? Any chutney can be pureed in a blender or food processor to turn it into a ketchup! And

remember that ketchup doesn't have to be tomato based: Any fruit or vegetable that makes good chutney will be delicious as a ketchup.

4. Sandwich booster: Combine equal parts mayonnaise and chutney and spread it on one of the slices of bread before building the rest of the sandwich with whatever main ingredients you wish. You can leave the chutney spread chunky, or puree it for a smooth texture.

5. Under the grilled cheese: Lightly toast bread, then spread a layer of chutney on it. Top that with a sharp cheddar or other tangy cheese and broil the open-faced sandwich until the cheese melts. For an hors d'oeuvre version, use crackers instead of the toast. Serve hot.

6. Tempura dipping sauce: In a small saucepan, combine a heaping tablespoon of chutney with ¼ cup chicken, vegetable, or fish stock, 1 tablespoon mirin or other sweet white wine, 1 teaspoon soy sauce, and ½ teaspoon grated fresh ginger. Bring to a simmer over medium heat and serve hot with tempura vegetables. You can also puree the ingredients for a smooth sauce and then heat them just before serving.

7. Glaze for roasting: Purée chutney with a little water in a food processor or blender. Brush the glaze on meat or poultry before roasting.

8. With game meats and lamb: These don't have to be curried to benefit from a spoonful of chutney. Simply serve the chutney as a condiment alongside any richly flavored meat such as venison or lamb.

9. Chutney salsa: Combine equal parts any kind of salsa and chutney. Stir in finely chopped cilantro (coriander leaves) or parsley. Taste and see if maybe it needs a pinch of salt (it may not if the salsa was a very salty one). Serve with tortilla chips.

10. With roasted root vegetables or winter squash: Preheat the oven to 400°F. Scrub the root vegetables clean and peel them (the peeling is optional). Chop them into 1-inch chunks. Peel and seed the winter squash and cut the flesh into 1-inch chunks. Mix the root vegetable and winter squash pieces together with chutney in a large mixing bowl. Use approximately ¼ cup of chutney for 2 pounds of vegetables. When well mixed, spread the combination on a lightly greased roasting pan. Roast until the vegetables are easily pierced with a fork, 30 to 40 minutes.

Sweet Red Pepper and Cucumber Relish

PREP TIME: 15 minutes   COOKING TIME: 20 minutes   SALTING TIME: 8–12 hours
YIELD: 4 half-pint jars; recipe can be doubled

This particular recipe combines the sunny color of southern-style sweet pepper relish with another classic, cucumber hot dog relish. But don't just use it on hot dogs. It is also fabulous in deviled eggs and potato salad.

INGREDIENTS

2 Cucumbers

3 large red bell peppers

2 medium-large onions

2 tablespoons kosher or medium-grain sea salt

1½ teaspoons cornstarch

½ cup apple cider vinegar

¾ cup sugar or ½ cup light honey (orange blossom, clover, or wildflower honey works well)

½ teaspoon celery seeds

½ teaspoon turmeric

⅛ teaspoon freshly ground nutmeg

⅛ teaspoon freshly ground black pepper

HOW TO MAKE RELISH

Relish is basically a finely chopped pickle, usually a sweet-and-sour one, that is used as a condiment on other dishes (think hot dog relish). The basic recipe below can be used with zucchini, beets, and other vegetables to make delicious relish variations.

INSTRUCTIONS

1. Wash the cucumbers. Slice off the stem ends and compost or discard them. Peel the cucumbers (you can skip this for a red-and-green-colored relish, but peeling the cukes results in a relish with a lovely rosy color). Cut the cucumbers in half lengthwise. If they are very seedy, use a small spoon to scoop out and compost or discard the seeds. Finely chop the cucumbers, or pulse them a few times in a food processor. You want them to be minced, not pureed.

2. Slice off the stems of the red bell peppers. Cut them in half and remove the seeds and any white pith. Peel the onions and slice off the ends. Finely chop the red peppers and onions, or pulse them a few times in a food processor. As with the cucumbers, you want them to be minced, not puréed.

3. Combine the cucumbers, sweet peppers, and onions in a large bowl. Add the salt and mix well. Don't worry if it seems like a lot of salt—you'll be rinsing most of it off in the next step. The salt will draw water out of the vegetables, which will result in better taste and texture in the finished relish.

   Cover the bowl of salted vegetables and leave it in the refrigerator overnight or for 8 to 12 hours.

4. Put the vegetables into a finely meshed sieve and let them drain for a couple of minutes. Rinse them under cold water and then let them drain again for another minute or two. Press on the vegetables with the back of a wooden spoon or your clean hands to remove as much liquid as possible.

5. In a large pot, whisk the cornstarch into the apple cider vinegar. Add the sugar or honey and the spices, and bring the mixture to a boil over medium heat, stirring to dissolve the sugar or honey.

6. Once the spiced vinegar syrup is boiling, add the minced vegetables. Bring the mixture back to a boil, then reduce the heat and simmer, stirring occasionally, for 10 minutes.

7. Spoon the relish into clean, hot canning jars. Press down on the relish with the back of a spoon or your clean fingers to release any air bubbles. Leave ½ inch of head space. Screw on the canning lids and process the relish in a boiling water bath for 10 minutes (adjust the canning time if you live at a high altitude—see the Boiling Water Bath Canning chapter). Once it's been canned in a boiling water bath, the relish will keep inside the sealed jars at room temperature for at least a year. Once opened, the relish will keep in the refrigerator for up to 3 months.

8. Wait at least a week for the flavors to mingle and develop before serving the relish.

HOW TO SAFELY USE HOMEMADE VINEGAR IN PICKLING

You may have read elsewhere that it is not safe to use homemade vinegar in pickling. That's not strictly true. It is not safe to use vinegars that contain less than 4.5 percent acetic acid (or to dilute the vinegar with more water than the recipe specifies). So if you know the pH of your homemade vinegar, and it is acidic enough, there is no reason not to use it.

You can figure out the percentage of acetic acid in homemade vinegar with something called an acid titration kit, available from winemaking supply companies (see Useful Resources). The process for testing for acetic acid is slightly different from the instructions the kit comes with for testing wine acidity. Here's how you do it (all of the tools and solutions come with the kit).

1. Use the 20ml syringe that comes with the kit to measure 2ml of homemade vinegar and transfer that to the testing cup.

2. Add 20ml of water and 3 drops of the indicator solution. Stir to combine.

3. Fill the syringe with 10ml of the standard base solution. Add it to the mixture in the testing cup 1ml at a time. Stir after each addition. At first, the solution will be clear, but eventually it will turn dark pink. Stop adding standard base when that happens.

4. Look at the syringe that held the 10ml of standard base and note how much you used up. For instance, if there is 2ml left, then you used 8ml.

5. Multiply the number of milliliters of standard base you added by 0.6. The result is the percentage of acetic acid in your homemade vinegar. For example, if you used 8ml of standard base, multiply 8 by 0.6 and you get 4.8. A vinegar with 4.8 percent acetic acid is safe to use for pickling!

Note that you are testing the acetic acid percentage here, not the pH. It could be confusing because with acetic acid testing, the higher the percentage number, the more acidic the vinegar. But with pH testing, *lower* numbers equal greater acidity.

Apple Scrap Vinegar

PREP TIME: 5 minutes   FERMENTATION TIME: 1 week   YIELD: 1 pint

---

When you make applesauce, pie, or any apple recipe, save the cores (and the peels if the apples were organically grown). Use them for this incredibly easy method of making vinegar. You can stockpile the apple scraps in the freezer until you have enough.

INGREDIENTS

2–3 tablespoons sugar

2–3 cups filtered or non-chlorinated water

1 pound apple cores and peels (peels only if from organically grown apples)

INSTRUCTIONS

1. Use 1 tablespoon of the sugar per cup of water. Dissolve the sugar in the water. It is important to use non-chlorinated or filtered water because chlorine could prevent the fermentation process that is essential to making vinegar.

2. Put the apple scraps into a ceramic, glass, or stainless-steel bowl, pot, or crock and pour the sugar water over them. Use enough of the liquid to cover the apples, but don't worry if they float a bit.

3. Cover with a clean dish towel and let sit at room temperature for 1 week. Every day, stir the ingredients vigorously at least once (more is better). Once fermentation begins, the liquid will froth up when you stir it.

4. The liquid should have started to turn a darker color after one week of steeping and stirring. Strain out the fruit.

5. Keep the liquid at room temperature, stirring once or more each day, for 2 weeks to 1 month. Its smell will shift from lightly alcoholic to vinegary and sour. The bacteria that create vinegar from alcohol require oxygen to do so. That's why it's important not to cover the liquid with anything airtight during the process. (FYI, *all* vinegar starts out as alcohol—it's what the bacteria that make vinegar eat.)

6. Once the vinegar tastes as strong as you'd like it, transfer it to bottles and screw on covers or cork. The vinegar is fine to use for salad dressings, marinades, and sauces anytime it tastes good to you. But if you want to use your homemade vinegar for safe pickling and canning, it needs to have at least 4.5 percent acetic acid, just like commercial brands do.

CHAPTER FOUR

Sweet Preserves

Jams, jellies, preserves, conserves, marmalades, fruit butters, and syrups are the sweet "something extra" we treat ourselves to. Just a dollop turns toast into breakfast, pancakes into a feast.

So what *are* the differences among these types of sweet condiments? A jam contains pieces of the fruit it is made with, whereas a jelly uses the fruit's juice only and doesn't include even a speck of pulp. Although any sweet fruit spread may be called a preserve, technically if you call it preserves instead of jam that means it is made with whole small fruits such as cherries or blueberries rather than chopped fruit—but even commercial brands use the names *jam* and *preserve* interchangeably. A conserve is like a jam or preserve except that it includes dried fruits and nuts. Marmalades are made with citrus and include slivers of the peels. Fruit butters are simply fruit purées such as applesauce cooked down to a spreadable consistency. Syrups are sweet pourable liquids.

What Makes It Safe?

Sweet preserves don't have to contain sugar, but those made with sugar keep longer than sugar-free products. Despite that, the sugar in fruit preserves isn't the main thing that preserves them safely. Sugar has a fairly neutral pH of 7 and so cannot lower the pH of a recipe sufficiently to inhibit the growth of harmful bacteria. Instead, it's the acidity of the fruit that does that. Even though sweet preserves may be processed in a boiling water bath to seal the jars and prevent mold, the acidity of the ingredients is the main thing safely preserving the food. Because fruits are acidic foods on the pH scale, they may be safely canned in a boiling water bath.

Although sugar only contributes marginally

to the preservation of sweet preserves, what sugar *does* do is bond with the pectin in fruit to create a gel. That's why if you reduce the sugar below what is called for in a jelly recipe, you may end up with something too runny to spread on toast (just call it syrup and use it on your pancakes instead). Sugar dissolved at high heat in the presence of acid and pectin is what creates the glistening, soft, but not liquid texture we expect from most sweet preserves.

MAKING LOW- OR NO-SUGAR PRESERVES

In order to get a good gel in jams, jellies, and other sweet preserves with very little or no sugar, you need to use a special kind of low-methoxyl pectin. If you order a low-methoxyl pectin such as the one in Useful Resources, it will come with a packet of calcium powder and detailed instructions for use. The low-methoxyl pectin and the calcium powder work in combination to enable even sugar-free recipes to gel.

I highly recommend low-methoxyl pectin if you need to reduce sugar in your diet. However, the texture of preserves made with this product is not identical to those made with sugar. For example, sugar-free jelly made with low-methoxyl pectin can have a consistency closer to Jell-O than jelly.

Pectin is a naturally occurring substance found in most fruits. There is more pectin in underripe fruits than in ripe, and some fruits are naturally higher in pectin than others. If you are working with a low-pectin fruit such as strawberries, you have three choices: You can either add pectin, combine the low-pectin fruit with a high-pectin fruit, or cook the heck out of the low-pectin fruit until enough moisture evaporates away that your jam thickens. That last option destroys so much of the color and flavor of fruit that I do not recommend it.

HIGH- AND LOW-PECTIN FRUIT

When you look up the fruit that you want to pre-serve, remember that that if it's on the low-pectin list you will either need to add pectin or combine it with a high-pectin fruit.

Most commercial pectins come in either powder or liquid form and are made from either apple or cit-rus pectin. I am not a big fan of these, because most recipes that use commercial pectins require huge amounts of sugar. You end up just tasting the sugar, not the fruit. Fortunately, it is quite easy to make your own pectin, and homemade pectin can be used with significantly less sugar in preserves.

HIGH-PECTIN FRUITS	LOW-PECTIN FRUITS
Apples	Apricots
Citrus rinds & seeds	Blackberries
Crab apples	Blueberries
Cranberries	Cherries
Currants	Elderberries
Gooseberries	Peaches
Plums	Pears
Grapes	Pineapple
Quinces	Raspberries
	Strawberries

Homemade Apple Pectin

PREP TIME: 10 minutes   COOKING TIME: 1 hour   OVERNIGHT STRAINING: 8 hours

YIELD: approximately 1 pint

Most of the pectin in apples is concentrated in the skins and cores of the fruit. Tart apples have much more pectin than sweet ones. You can save the skins and cores of tart apples in the freezer until you've stockpiled enough to make this pectin recipe. Be sure to use organically grown apples so that you don't end up with pesticides in your preserves.

INGREDIENTS

2 quarts apple peels and cores *or* whole apples chopped into 1-inch chunks

2 tablespoons lemon juice

Water

INSTRUCTIONS

1. Put the apple scraps and lemon juice into a large, nonreactive pot. Add water to not quite cover.

2. Bring the ingredients to a boil over high heat. Reduce the heat and simmer, stirring occasionally, until the apple cores become mushy. This can take up to 1 hour.

3. Place a jelly bag or a colander lined with several layers of cheesecloth over a large bowl. Pour the apples and their cooking liquid into the bag or the cheesecloth-lined colander. Leave this to strain overnight or 8 hours. Do not squeeze the bag to hurry the process. If you do, your homemade pectin will make any jellies you use it in cloudy.

4. The slightly thick liquid that strains through is your homemade apple pectin. You should have about a quart of it. Boil this down until it is reduced by half.

5. Store any pectin you are not using right away in the freezer, or can it in half-pint jars in a boiling water bath for 10 minutes.

Homemade Citrus Pectin

PREP TIME: 15 minutes   COOKING TIME: 15 minutes   MACERATION TIME: 3 hours   YIELD: 1 cup

The white pith just under the skins of citrus fruit is high in pectin. Any citrus fruit can be used, but choose ones that have a thick layer of white pith for good results with this recipe. The seeds are also high in pectin, so use those as well.

Homemade citrus pectin can have a faint bitterness from the white piths. Use it in recipes that contain spices or strongly flavored fruits.

INGREDIENTS

½ pound white parts of citrus peels plus any seeds

¼ cup lemon juice

2 cups water

INSTRUCTIONS

1. Use a zester or a vegetable peel to remove the colorful skins of the citrus fruit. These are aromatic and flavorful, so you may want to save them for another use. But they don't bring any pectin to the party and could overwhelm the other flavors in your recipe.

2. Peel or cut off the remaining white layer of the fruits. Remove and set aside any seeds. Save the

pulp for another use. Finely chop the white parts and weigh them; you'll need 8 ounces.

3. Put the chopped citrus peel pith, seeds, and the lemon juice in a nonreactive, medium-sized pot. Cover and leave at room temperature for 2 hours. Add the water and leave at room temperature for 1 more hour.

4. Bring the ingredients to a boil, uncovered, over high heat. Reduce the heat and simmer for 15 minutes. Remove from the heat and let cool to room temperature.

5. Strain through a jelly bag or through a colander lined with several layers of cheesecloth. Return the liquid to a pot over high heat and boil until it reduces by half.

6. Store any homemade citrus pectin that you will not be using right away in the freezer, or can it in half-pint jars in a boiling water bath for 10 minutes (adjust the canning time if you live at a high altitude—see the sidebar in the Boiling Water Bath Canning chapter).

The Gel Point

When you're making any kind of sweet preserve except syrup or fruit butter, the ingredients are boiled at high heat until the mixture reaches the gel point. This is not something you can judge simply by looking at the food while it cooks. If you are making jelly, for instance, it will still be entirely liquid when it reaches the gel point, and only thicken as it cools. If you cook that jelly until it starts to thicken while still in the cooking pot over heat, you'll end up with candy instead of jelly.

The gel point occurs at 220°F, which is 8°F above the temperature of boiling water. In theory, you can use a candy thermometer or a digital thermometer to tell when your ingredients have reached that temperature. In practice, I've had mixed results relying on a thermometer and recommend using other methods to test for the gel point.

As your sweet preserve boils, keep an eye on the size of the bubbles. At first they will be small. As the preserve nears the gel point, the bubbles will get bigger and begin to climb the sides of the pot. When they do so, start testing for the gel point using one of the methods below.

By the way, the fact that the bubbles on the surface of your boiling preserve will eventually climb the sides of a pot is why it is rarely a good idea to double a jam or jelly recipe. You need several inches of space between the surface of the food and the top of the pot or you will end up with gooey sweet stuff all over your stove!

THE WRINKLE TEST

While the preserve is cooking, keep a small plate in the freezer. To test for the gel point, put a small amount of the preserve—about 1/2 teaspoon—on the plate and return it to the freezer for 1 minute. Remove the pot from the heat while you are doing this so that you don't risk overshooting the gel point by continuing to cook the preserve. Take the plate out of the freezer and use a finger to push the dab of preserve sideways on the plate. If the preserve wrinkles when you do this, it has reached the gel point.

I usually use the wrinkle test as a backup to the spoon test. Once the spoon test reaches the sheeting stage, I use the wrinkle test just to confirm that the preserve I'm making has gotten to the gel point.

THE SPOON TEST

Dip a large spoon into the pot, filling it with the still-boiling preserve. Lift the spoon about a foot above the pot, and immediately pour the spoonful of jelly or other preserve back into the pot. Carefully observe how the last drop or drops pour off the edge of the spoon. In the early stages of cooking your preserve, the last bit to pour off will be a single drop. As it nears the gel point, the last bit to come off the spoon will split into two drops. When it finally reaches the gel point, those two drops will run together and come off the spoon in a gloppy "sheet" (which is why the gel point is sometimes called the sheeting point). Immediately remove the pot from the heat at this point and follow the recipe instructions for canning.

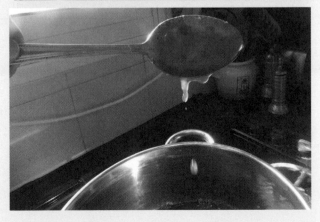

Strawberry Jam

PREP TIME: 10 minutes   COOKING TIME: 25–35 minutes   MACERATION TIME: 8 hours

YIELD: 3 to 4 half-pint jars

This recipe works with any low-pectin fruit, but is especially wonderful with strawberries. It is made with homemade pectin and uses less sugar than is called for in most recipes that use commercial pectin. It also doesn't need to be cooked as long. The secret is the overnight maceration, and the result is a brightly colored and flavored jam that does honor to the fruit. Frozen fruit works just as well as fresh in this recipe, assuming that the fruit was top quality before it was frozen.

You can also use this recipe for high-pectin fruit. Just leave out the homemade pectin and skip the overnight maceration.

INGREDIENTS

4 pounds ripe strawberries

2½ cups sugar

½ cup homemade apple or citrus pectin

2 tablespoons bottled lemon juices

INSTRUCTIONS

1. Rinse off the strawberries under cool water. Cut off their green hulls and compost or discard. Slice the strawberries into halves or quarters (you can leave very small ones whole).

2. Combine the strawberries and the sugar in a large pot. Stir gently to combine. Cover the pot and put it into the refrigerator for 8 to 10 hours. The sugar will draw out the liquid from the strawberries so that they are macerating in their own juices.

3. Sterilize the canning jars (see the Boiling Water Bath Canning chapter).

4. Put the pot with the strawberry-and-sugar mixture on the stove over high heat. Stir to liquefy any sugar that has not yet dissolved. Add the homemade pectin and the lemon juice. Cook, stirring often, until the jam reaches the gel point.

5. Ladle the jam into the sterilized canning jars. Leave ½-inch head space. Wipe the rims of the jars clean. Screw on the canning lids.

6. Process in a boiling water bath for 5 minutes. Adjust processing time for high altitude accordingly.

HOW TO MAKE JELLY

A basic recipe for any jelly is 1 part sugar for every 1 to 2 parts fruit juice, plus 1 tablespoon of lemon juice per cup of juice (you can skip the lemon juice with very tart fruit such as crab apples). If the fruit the juice is made from is on the low-pectin list, add ¼ cup homemade pectin per cup of juice. Measure the combined pectin and juice then calculate how much sugar and lemon juice to add based on the ratio above. Follow the cooking and canning instructions in the following recipe.

Apple Scrap Jelly

COOKING TIME: 45 minutes   PROCESSING TIME: 5 minutes

YIELD: 2 to 3 half-pint jars

The next time you are making applesauce or apple pie, save the cores for this "something for nothing" jelly. If you've got organically grown apples, save the peels as well (but only if they're organic—you don't want pesticides in your jelly). You can stockpile the scraps in the freezer until you have enough.

It's easiest to get to the gel point with this recipe if you use lightly underripe or tart apples because they contain more pectin than sweeter apples. Including a few peels from red apples will impart a beautiful blush color to the jelly.

INGREDIENTS

Cores of 12–15 apples, plus peels if the apples are organically grown

Water

1½ cups sugar

3 tablespoons bottled lemon juice

INSTRUCTIONS

1. Sterilize the half-pint jars.

2. Put the apple cores and peels into a large nonreactive pot and add just enough water to cover them. Bring to a boil and cook the apple scraps until the liquid has reduced by half. The cores should be very mushy by this point.

3. Strain the solids out of the mixture, reserving the liquid. Measure the liquid and put it back into the pot. Add ½ cup of sugar and 1 tablespoon of lemon juice for every cup of apple liquid.

4. Bring the ingredients to a boil over high heat, stirring often. When the mixture reaches the gel point, remove the hot jelly from the heat and immediately pour it into the sterilized jars. Leave ½ inch of head space between the surface of the jelly and the rims of the jars. Wipe the rims clean and screw on the canning lids.

5. Process in a boiling water bath for 5 minutes. Adjust the canning time if you live at a high altitude (see the *Boiling Water Bath Canning* chapter).

Slow-Cooker Pear Butter

PREP TIME: 5 minutes   CANNING TIME: 20 minutes
YIELD: 2 half-pint jars

This pear butter has rich flavor and a silky-smooth texture. I like it swirled into yogurt for breakfast, and also use it as an ingredient in quick breads. The recipe works equally well with apples, plums, and other fruit..

INGREDIENTS

2 pounds ripe pears

⅓ cup water

Juice and grated zest of 1 lemon

3 tablespoons honey or ¼ cup brown sugar (optional)

INSTRUCTIONS

1. Peel and core the pears. The grittiness that pears can sometimes have is concentrated just under the peels, so peeling the fruit makes a big difference in the texture of your final product.

2. Cut the peeled and cored pears into 1-inch chunks.

3. Put the pears, water, lemon, and honey or sugar (if using) into a slow cooker. Cover and cook on high for 4 to 5 hours. The pears should become very soft.

4. Transfer the pears to a blender or food processor using a slotted spoon. Reserve the cooking liquid

HOW TO
MAKE FRUIT BUTTER

Fruit butters can be made from any fruit puree. Cooking the fruit gently in a slow cooker for a long time results in a smoother fruit butter, and also means you don't have to spend your time standing over the stove stirring.

SPICED PEAR BUTTER

Tie cinnamon sticks, a couple of whole cloves, and a few whole allspice berries in cheesecloth. Add the spice bundle to the slow cooker with the other ingredients, and remove it before you purée the fruit. Do not use ground spices—they turn bitter during the long time in the slow cooker.

SPIKED PEAR BUTTER

Try adding a dash of cognac or tawny port to the other ingredients.

left in the slow cooker. Purée the pears. Add the cooking liquid as necessary to achieve a thick but spreadable consistency.

5. Spoon the pear butter into clean half- or quarter-pint canning jars. Use a butter knife or a spoon to press out any air bubbles. Leave ½ inch of head space. Wipe the rims of the jars clean and screw on the canning lids.

6. Process in a boiling water bath for 20 minutes (adjust the time for your altitude if necessary; see the Boiling Water Bath Canning chapter).

Fig Preserves with Wine and Balsamic Vinegar

PREP TIME: 10 minutes   COOKING TIME: 15 minutes   MACERATION TIME: 1 hour   YIELD: 4 half-pint jars

The splash of red wine and dash of balsamic vinegar in this recipe balance the rich sweetness of the figs perfectly. Don't just eat these preserves on toast: Serve them with goat cheese, a crusty bread, and the rest of that bottle of red wine you opened to use in the recipe.

INGREDIENTS

3 pounds fresh, ripe figs

1¼ cups sugar

1 cup honey

½ cup dry red wine

¼ cup balsamic vinegar

INSTRUCTIONS

1. Wash the figs and slice off the stems. Leave very small figs whole, or cut them in half. Cut larger figs into quarters.

2. Put the figs with the other ingredients in a large nonreactive pot. Stir gently to combine. Cover the pot and leave the ingredients at room temperature for 1 to 2 hours.

3. Take off the cover. Bring the fig mixture to a boil over high heat, stirring frequently.

4. Once the jam begins to thicken, stir constantly to prevent it from sticking to the bottom of the pot and burning. Test for the gel point frequently at this stage.

5. As soon as the jam reaches the gel point, remove it from the heat. Ladle the jam into clean canning jars (it is not necessary to sterilize the jars for this recipe). Leave ½ inch of head space between the surface of the food and the rims of the jars. Wipe the rims clean. Screw on the canning lids.

6. Process in a boiling water bath for 15 minutes. Adjust the canning time if you live at a high altitude (see the sidebar in the Boiling Water Bath Canning chapter).

Jellied Cranberry Sauce with Spicebush and Orange

PREP TIME: 5 minutes   COOKING TIME: 15 minutes   CANNING TIME: 5 minutes
YIELD: 1 to 2 half-pint jars; recipe can be doubled

This holiday treat has gorgeous color and flavor. It also slides out of its jar ready to be sliced—built-in presentation! If you don't have spicebush (*Lindera benzoin*), you can substitute a combination of black pepper and allspice as I suggest in the recipe.

Note that although I usually prefer less sugar than this when I make whole cranberry sauce, for this recipe it's best not to reduce the sugar or you might not get a solid enough gel.

INGREDIENTS

Juice and zest of 1 organically grown orange

12 ounces whole cranberries

½–¾ cup water

1 cup sugar

1 cinnamon stick

6 lightly crushed spicebush berries or 2 black peppercorns plus 4 whole allspice berries

INSTRUCTIONS

1. Sterilize the canning jars (see the Boiling Water Bath Canning chapter).

2. Grate the zest of the orange with a microplane or the fine-holed side of a box grater, removing only the aromatic orange outer layer and none of the bitter white pith. It is important to use an organically grown orange when you are going to use the zest. Reserve the zest.

3. Cut the zested orange in half. Squeeze the juice into a measuring cup, being sure to strain out any seeds. Add water to make a total of 1 cup liquid.

4. Put the cup of liquid, the cranberries, and the sugar into a pot on the stove. Tie the spices into a cheesecloth bundle and add them to the other ingredients.

5. Bring the ingredients to a boil over high heat, stirring to dissolve the sugar. The cranberries will start to make popping sounds as they split open. Keep boiling them over high heat, stirring occasionally, until most of the cranberries have popped. Some of the cranberries may still look whole, but if they squish softly when you press them against the side of the pot with the back of a spoon, they've popped.

6. Once the cranberries have popped, cook the sauce for an additional 5 minutes. Turn off the heat. Remove and discard the spice bundle.

7. If you have a food mill, run the sauce through it to remove the cranberry skins. If you don't have a food mill, puree the sauce in a blender or food processor and then use the back of a spoon to press it through a sieve or fine-holed colander.

8. Whisk the orange zest into the sauce.

9. Spoon the sauce into the sterilized jars, leaving ½ inch of head space. Wipe the rims clean and secure the lids. Process in a boiling water bath for 5 minutes. Adjust processing time for high altitude accordingly.

   The sauce will still be very soft when you spoon it into the jars. It will firm up as it cools. Wait 24 hours before attempting to remove it from the jars in a single piece.

Kumquat Marmalade with Bourbon

PREP TIME: 30 minutes   COOKING TIME: 1 hour, 15 minutes   SOAKING TIME: 4 hours
YIELD: 5 to 6 half-pint jars

This method of making marmalade uses the natural pectin in the citrus peels, in combination with the sugar and the acidity of the lemon juice, to achieve a good gel. It's a labor-intensive recipe, I admit, but the bright color and taste of the marmalade is worth it, with or without the added dash of bourbon.

You can use this recipe with any citrus fruit.

INGREDIENTS

35–40 kumquats, 1–2 inches long and less than half as wide

1 orange

6–7 cups water

2–3 tablespoons bottled lemon juice

4–5 cups sugar

¼ cup bourbon (optional)

> ### NOTE
>
> Marmalades, more than most other sweet preserves, continue to thicken for days or even weeks after they've cooled in the jars. If your freshly made marmalade is not as thick as you would like it to be, wait 2 weeks and it may get to a firmer gel.

INSTRUCTIONS

1. Wash the kumquats and the orange, scrubbing them well with a produce brush.

2. Slice the fruits very thinly, peels and all. Remove and discard the seeds as you are slicing. You want the juices as well as the peels and pulp, so have a bowl handy to transfer them to.

3. Measure the combined sliced citrus and juices. Put them into a large, nonreactive pot. Stir in 2 cups water for every cup of fruit and juice that you measured. Cover the pot and let sit at room temperature for 4 hours (or overnight).

4. Near the end of the soaking time, sterilize your canning jars.

5. Bring the citrus-and-water mixture to a boil over high heat. Reduce the heat to medium and simmer until the kumquat and orange peels become tender and translucent. This will take about an hour.

6. Once the fruit mixture has cooked, measure it. Add 1½ teaspoons lemon juice plus ¾ cup sugar for every cup of cooked citrus. Stir the ingredients over high heat until the sugar dissolves.

7. Add the bourbon, if using. Continue to cook over high heat until the marmalade reaches the gel point. Remove it from the heat and skim off any foam on the surface.

8. While the marmalade is still hot, ladle it into the sterilized canning jars. Leave a minimum of 1/2 inch head space between the surface of the food and the rims of the jars. Screw on the canning lids.

9. Process in a boiling water bath for 5 minutes (adjust for your altitude if necessary; see the Boiling Water Bath Canning chapter).

Cherry Syrup

PREP TIME: 30 minutes COOKING TIME: 20 minutes CANNING TIME: 10 minutes
YIELD: Depends on how much juice you use

Syrup isn't just for pancakes!
Try using fruit syrups as cocktail flavorings, or drizzle them over fruit salads, yogurt, or cake. This recipe is a great prototype for turning any fruit into a delicious, versatile syrup.

1. What stands between you and perfect cherry syrup is the pits. There are a few ways to deal with them:

   If you have a high-quality juicing machine that can handle the pits, use that to extract the juice.

   If you don't have a juicer, you can use the hot water extraction method. Simply pierce each cherry with the tip of a paring knife to encourage the juices to escape. Put the cherries in a pot and add water to not-quite cover them. Bring to a boil over high heat. Reduce the heat and simmer until the color (and flavor) has gone out of the fruit and into the water, about 20 minutes. You can add a little more water if necessary to keep the fruit not-quite-fully immersed in the liquid while it is simmering. Strain out the solids, reserving the liquid to make your syrup.

   Here's the laziest but also excellent method: Buy some unsweetened cherry (or other fruit) juice.

   Once you've gotten some fruit juice by any of the methods above:

2. Measure the fruit juice. Add 2 parts sugar or 1½ parts honey to 1 part juice.

3. Cook the mixture over low heat, stirring, until the sugar or honey is completely dissolved. Measure the mixture and add 1 tablespoon lemon juice per pint of syrup.

4. Fruit syrup will keep in the refrigerator for 3 months. It can be frozen for at least 6 months. For longer-term storage at room temperature, can pint jars of fruit syrup in a boiling water bath for 10 minutes. Adjust the canning time if you live at a high altitude (see the Boiling Water Bath Canning chapter).

Violet Flower Syrup

PREP TIME: 15 minutes   COOKING TIME: 10 minutes   OVERNIGHT INFUSION: 24 hours

YIELD: 2 cups

Violet plants only produce their edible flowers (*Viola species*) for a few weeks in early spring. With its amethyst color and subtle flavor, this syrup preserves them for year-round enjoyment.

Variations: You can use this method with linden blossoms, elderflowers, cherry blossoms, and other edible flowers, as well as aromatic leaves including sassafras and mint.

INGREDIENTS

1 cup lightly packed violet flowers (no stems)

1 cup boiling water

2 cups sugar

INSTRUCTIONS

1. Pinch off the stems under each violet. You may want to save these for a salad: They are edible and quite tasty, but don't add color to the syrup. Remove the calyces (the green bases of the flowers).

2. Put the violet petals into a heatproof glass or stainless-steel container (a canning jar works perfectly).

3. Bring the water to a boil. Pour the hot water

over the violet petals. Cover and let sit at room temperature for 24 hours. The liquid will turn a beautiful blue-amethyst color.

4. Pour the liquid and the petals into the top of a bain-marie (double boiler). You can make a bain-marie by putting an inch or two of water in a pot over medium-high heat and setting a large stainless-steel or other heatproof bowl on top of the pot. Put the violets and their infusion into the bowl.

5. Add the sugar and cook the syrup over the steam created by the bain-marie, stirring often, until the sugar is completely dissolved. If it does not, add 1 tablespoon of lemon juice. Note: It

is important to use only granulated white sugar for this recipe or you'll lose the exquisite color.

6. Strain the syrup through a finely meshed sieve to remove the flower petals. Let the syrup cool to room temperature then transfer it to glass jars, and label them. Violet flower syrup is not recommended for boiling water bath canning. Instead, store the syrup in the refrigerator. Violet flower syrup will keep, refrigerated, for at least 6 months.

Lemon Curd

COOKING TIME: 5 minutes   COOKING TIME: 30 minutes   CANNING TIME: 15 minutes

YIELD: 3 half-pint jars

A fruit curd is a creamy concoction rich with eggs, butter, and bright fruit flavor. I had a friend who used to show up at Christmas with jars of her homemade lemon curd. It was rich, but the citrus juice kept it from being cloying. I think it was my dad who figured out that a dollop of lemon curd served on top of a gingersnap cookie is a first-rate dessert or snack. My friend's lemon curd hooked me on this creamy treat, and I've been making fruit curds ever since she introduced me to them.

Curds can be made with other fruits, including not only other kinds of citrus but also passionfruit, raspberries, and any other juicy, slightly tart fruit.

INGREDIENTS

Zest from 2 lemons

½ cup fresh lemon juice (that's about what you'll get from 3–5 lemons)

2 large eggs plus the yolk from a third egg

½ cup sugar

7 tablespoons butter (slightly less than one 8-ounce stick)

INSTRUCTIONS

1. Grate the zest from the 2 lemons and reserve. Cut the zested lemons in half crosswise and squeeze out the juice into a measuring cup, being careful to strain out any seeds. Juice additional lemons as needed to bring the amount of juice up to ½ cup.

6. Continue whisking until the sugar is utterly dissolved and the butter completely melted. Put aside the whisk and switch to a wooden spoon. Stir frequently (every 30 seconds at least, but it doesn't have to be constantly) until the curd begins to thicken. This will take about 10 or 15 minutes.

7. Once the curd starts to thicken, no more walking away from the stove. You're on duty: Stir nonstop until the curd is thick enough to richly coat the back of the wooden spoon you're stirring with. If you stop stirring, you'll end up with a texture closer to scrambled eggs than the smooth, buttery goodness you're after.

   You can test the doneness of the lemon curd by putting a tiny dollop of it on a cold plate (put the plate in the freezer for a minute). The curd should set up to a consistency something like a pudding or custard. If it doesn't, keep cooking and stirring a little longer, remembering that the hot mixture in the pot will be more liquid than the final curd.

2. In a separate bowl, beat the whole eggs and the extra egg yolk together.

3. Put an inch or two of water into the bottom part of a double boiler (you can improvise a double boiler by putting a heatproof bowl over the top of a pot that is smaller than the bowl). Bring the water to a boil.

4. Add the beaten eggs to the top part of the double boiler. Add the sugar and stir to combine.

5. Add the lemon juice and zest to the egg-sugar mixture and stir well. Add the butter in small chunks. Use a whisk to work each bit of butter in, waiting until each chunk completely melts before adding the next.

8. Spoon the curd into clean canning jars, leaving ½ inch of head space. Run a table knife around the sides between the lemon curd and the jar to remove any air bubbles. Wipe the rims of the jars clean with a moist cloth or paper towel.

9. Screw the canning lids on finger-tight. Fruit curds will keep in the refrigerator without processing for up to 2 weeks. For longer storage, process the jars in a boiling water bath for 15 minutes. Adjust the canning time if you live at a high altitude (see the Pressure Canning chapter).

Candied Grapefruit Peels

PREP TIME: 10 minutes   COOKING TIME: 3 hours   DRAINING & COOLING TIME: 5 hours
YIELD: Approximately 1 quart

My grandmother used to make these. I loved everything about them when I was a kid, from the aromatic peels to the soft, moist centers and the gritty texture of the crystallized sugar coating.

For the best results, don't bother saving thin grapefruit peels. Use thick-skinned grapefruits with plenty of white pith. Although it is usually discarded as bitter and undesirable, that thick, white, spongy layer is exactly what you want for this recipe. And the candying process eliminates any bitterness.

Don't be daunted by the number of hours it takes to make candied grapefruit peels: most of that is inactive time, and once you're done this treat will keep at room temperature indefinitely. The fact that it keeps well at room temperature, and that grapefruits are in season in late fall and early winter, makes this an excellent holiday gift to send via snail mail.

INGREDIENTS

Peels from 4 large grapefruits

Water

3½ cups sugar, divided

INSTRUCTIONS

1. You don't have to go out and buy grapefruit specially for this recipe. Just eat some, or juice some, and save the peels in a bag or a sealed container in the crisper drawer of your refrigerator until you have enough for this recipe. The peels will keep in the refrigerator for up to 3 weeks, so you've got time to collect them. Scrape out any pulp or membranes with a spoon before storing the peels or proceeding with the recipe.

2. Most likely you sliced your grapefruits in half before eating or juicing them, and so you're starting with the peels of 8 grapefruit halves. Slice these into ½-inch-wide strips that are as long as the diameter of the grapefruit half.

3. Put the pieces of grapefruit peel into a large nonreactive pot (no aluminum, copper, or non-enameled cast iron, which could cause the preserve to discolor). Add enough water to cover the strips of peel by 1 inch (the peels will float—press down on them with a spoon to estimate the appropriate water level). Bring the water to a boil over high heat. As soon as the water reaches a boil, drain the grapefruit peels in a colander.

4. Put the drained grapefruit peel slices back into the pot and once again cover them with water. Bring to a boil over high heat as before, and once again remove the peels from the heat and drain them in a colander. Repeat this boil-and-drain process two more times (for a total of four times).

5. After you have boiled and drained the peels four times, put them back in the pot once again. Add 2½ cups of the sugar along with enough water to cover them by that same guesstimated inch as before. Bring the ingredients to a simmer over medium-high heat but do not let them reach a boil. Stir often to help the sugar dissolve. Once the sugar is completely dissolved, turn the heat down to low and simmer the peels, uncovered, for 2 hours.

6. The grapefruit peels will be very soft and translucent after simmering in the syrup. Let them cool to room temperature, still immersed in the syrup. If you need to take time out from your grapefruit-peel-candying project, now is the time to do it: The peels will keep at this stage, if soaking in the syrup and refrigerated, for up to 3 weeks.

7. Use tongs to lift each piece of grapefruit peel out of the syrup and transfer it to a rack set over a baking sheet. You won't be using any more of the syrup for this recipe, but it is very tasty and I recommend saving it for other concoctions (grapefruit syrup plus cold vodka is an excellent combination for a cocktail). Let the strips of grapefruit peel drain and dry for at least 4 hours or as long as 8 hours.

8. Spread 1 cup of sugar on a plate. Roll each piece of candied grapefruit peel in the sugar, coating it on all sides. Shake off any excess, and return the strip of peel to the rack over the baking sheet. Let dry for 1 to 4 hours more before storing the candied grapefruit peels. Don't pile them up or they'll stick together and get soggy: Instead, arrange them in single layers with waxed or parchment paper between each layer.

HOW TO CANDY FRUIT

This method can be used to candy small fruits like cherries and slices of larger fruits. But my favorite fruit candy is made from citrus peels.

CHAPTER FIVE

Pressure Canning

Although pressure canning also involves processing canning jars filled with food in hot water, it is a very different food preservation method from boiling water bath canning. Pressure canning enables you to can low-acid foods that could be dangerous if they were canned in a boiling water bath (seriously dangerous—think botulism). It also requires a pressure canner, which is a very specialized piece of equipment (and not the same as a pressure cooker).

Before we get into the specifics of how to use a pressure canner, I want to be sure you are entirely clear on which foods *must* be processed in a pressure canner and not a boiling water bath. Foods that are acidic (4.6 on the pH scale or lower) may be processed in a boiling water bath. As mentioned in the boiling water bath chapter, those foods include fruits and fruit preserves such as jam, as well as pickles and chutneys with a sufficient amount of vinegar in the recipe, and tomatoes (which are technically a fruit) with added acid.

But if you want to store more alkaline foods such as soup stocks, unpickled vegetables, or meat in sealed jars at room temperature, you must process them in a pressure canner. Here's why

Although *Clostridium botulinum* and the toxin it produces are killed at the temperature of boiling water, its spores can survive those temperatures. And guess what kind of environment they need in order to "hatch"? Someplace with moisture and without oxygen—exactly what they get inside sealed canning jars.

A pressure canner is capable of heating the food inside the jars to hotter than the temperature of boiling water, hot enough to kill off even the spores of botulism. That is why it is essential to use a pressure canner for low-acid foods.

What Is a Pressure Canner?

A pressure canner has a base that looks very much like a large metal pot, and a removable rack that fits into the base. The lid is where most of the gear is. A modern pressure canner's lid, which either screws on or is held in place with built-in clamps, has a steam vent (sometimes called a petcock) and either a weighted or a dial gauge that lets you know how many psig (pounds of pressure per square inch) have built up inside the canner.

Unlike some of their 20th-century predecessors, modern pressure canners have built-in safety fuses to release excess pressure well before it reaches a dangerous level.

Note that a pressure cooker is not the same piece of equipment as a pressure canner and cannot be used in its place, although a pressure *canner* can double as a pressure cooker.

How to Use a Pressure Canner

As with boiling water bath canning, when you fill canning jars with food for pressure canning it is important to leave a minimum of ½ inch head space. Wipe the rims of the jars clean before screwing on the canning lids. Note that it is never necessary to sterilize the jars before pressure canning since the processing time will always be longer than 10 minutes.

Place the rack that came with your pressure canner in the bottom of the canner. Add water. Unlike a boiling water bath, you will not completely cover the jars with water: Check the manufacturer's instructions for the specific amount to use for your model.

Secure the pressure canner's lid, leaving the vent open. Turn the heat on high. Eventually, steam will blow forcefully out of the vent. When it does so, set a timer for 10 minutes.

Once steam has been coming out of the vent for 10 minutes, close the vent. With a weighted gauge, you close the vent by covering it with the weight. The weight has three openings labeled with three different amounts of pressure: 5, 10, or 15. Use the opening for the number of pounds of pressure specified in the rec-

PRESSURE CANNING AT HIGH ALTITUDES

The fact that water boils at lower temperatures above sea level means that you need to adjust pressure canning instructions if you live at a high altitude. Instead of increasing the processing time as you do for boiling water bath canning at high altitudes, with pressure canning you keep the processing time but increase the pounds of pressure.

FOR WEIGHTED GAUGE PRESSURE CANNERS

Most pressure canning recipes call for processing at 10 PSIG. If you are using the kind of weighted gauge that shows 5–10–15, increase the pressure to the 15 PSIG level when pressure canning more than 1,000 feet above sea level.

FOR DIAL GAUGE PRESSURE CANNERS

Adjust the pressure by the following increments:

PRESSURE CANNING AT HIGH ALTITUDES	
ALTITUDE	INCREASE IN PSIG
1,001–3,000 feet	increase pressure by 2 PSIG
3,001–5,000 feet	increase pressure by 3 PSIG
5,001–7,000 feet	increase pressure by 4 PSIG
7,001+ feet	increase pressure by 5 PSIG

So for example, if a recipe tells you to pressure can your jars of food for 20 minutes at 10 PSIG but you live at 3,500 feet above sea level, you would still follow the 20-minute processing time, but increase the pressure to 13 PSIG.

ipe. When that level of pressure is reached, the gauge will begin to jiggle and release steam occasionally.

With a dial gauge, you simply read the pounds of pressure shown by the dial. Some pressure canner models have both a weighted and a dial gauge.

Once the inside of the canner reaches the desired amount of pressure, begin timing for the number of minutes given in the recipe.

Keep an eye on the pressure: If at any time it drops below the level called for, you have to bring the pressure back up and start timing all over again. For example, let's say I am canning a soup stock and the recipe calls for 20 minutes at 10 pounds pressure. But 15 minutes in I notice that the pressure has dropped to 8 pounds. I have to raise the heat and bring the pressure back up to 10 pounds, and then start timing the full 20 minutes all over again.

Once the canning time is done, turn off the heat but do not open the vent or try to take off the pressure canner's lid yet. Wait until the pressure in the canner drops down to zero, and then 2 more minutes after that.

After that waiting period is over, go ahead and open the vent and then the lid. Use a jar lifter to remove the jars to someplace where they can remain undisturbed until they are completely cooled (this can take several hours). If the surface you will be putting them on is cold, place a rack or dish towel there first and then the jars on top of that: Piping-hot glass jars touching a cold countertop can crack. It's not unusual for the contents of the jars to keep boiling vigorously for a few minutes after they come out of the pressure canner.

As the jars cool, the lids should go from flexible and convex to solid and concave, just as with boiling water bath canning. Resist the urge to test the lids before the jars of food have completely cooled: Pressing on them while still hot could create a false seal, meaning that a vacuum wasn't fully formed before the lid snapped into the concave position.

Pressure Canning Times for Vegetables

Here are the pressure canning instructions for the vegetables and fungi that hold up best to the canning process. I do not include potatoes or leafy greens here—although they may be safely pressure canned, the results are dismal. Cold storage or dehydrating are better choices for preserving potatoes, and freezing or dehydrating for leafy greens.

Most instructions for the hot pack method of pressure canning vegetables tell you to simply dump the blanched vegetables into a colander, wasting all that flavorful cooking liquid, and then cover the vegetables in the jars with plain boiling water. You could certainly do this. But you'll get a much tastier (and more nutritious) product if you follow the instructions I give below for using the liquid the vegetables blanched in as your canning liquid. It means taking a minute or two to remove the vegetables from the blanching liquid with a slotted spoon rather than dumping them into a colander, but it really is worth it.

ASPARAGUS

Remove the base ends of the asparagus. You may trim the remaining spears into 2-inch pieces or leave them longer, but be sure longer pieces are short enough to fit into the canning jars lengthwise with slightly more than an inch of head space above them.

Raw Pack

Pack raw asparagus spears tightly in clean, hot canning jars, leaving slightly more than 1 inch of head space. Pour boiling water over the asparagus, leaving 1 inch head space. Wipe the jar rims clean and secure the canning lids.

Hot Pack

Blanch asparagus in boiling water for 2 to 3 minutes. Use a slotted spoon to transfer the asparagus to clean, hot canning jars. Loosely fill the jars, leaving slightly more than 1 inch of head space. Pour the still-hot blanching liquid over the asparagus, leaving 1 inch head space. Wipe the jar rims clean and secure the canning lids.

Dial Gauge Canner

11 pounds; 30 minutes for pints, 40 for quarts. See the sidebar chart for high-altitude adjustments.

Weighted Gauge Canner

10 pounds; 30 minutes for pints, 40 for quarts. See the sidebar chart for high-altitude adjustments.

BEANS, REHYDRATED FROM DRY

This is important: You must rehydrate dry beans before canning them. To do so, either soak them in cool water overnight, or boil them for 2 minutes and then turn off the heat and let them soak in the hot water for 1 hour.

Either way, after the beans have soaked you need to boil them in fresh water for 30 minutes before canning them. I usually add a 2-inch piece of kombu

or wakame (types of dried seaweed) during this half hour of cooking. It doesn't change the flavor of the beans much, but it does add minerals—including iodine—and has a reputation for making the beans more tender.

The beans will finish cooking during their time in the pressure canner.

Hot Pack Only

Skim off and discard any foam that appeared while the beans were cooking. Use a slotted spoon to transfer the beans to clean, hot canning jars. Leave slightly more than 1 inch head space. Pour the hot cooking liquid over the beans, leaving 1 inch of head space. Wipe the jar rims clean and secure the canning lids.

Dial Gauge Canner

1 pounds; 75 minutes for pints, 90 for quarts. See the sidebar chart for high-altitude adjustments.

Weighted Gauge Canner

10 pounds; 75 minutes for pints, 90 for quarts. See the sidebar chart for high-altitude adjustments.

BEANS, GREEN AND WAX

Trim the stem ends off the beans. You may trim them into 2-inch pieces or leave them longer, but be sure longer pieces are short enough to fit into the canning jars lengthwise with slightly more than 1-inch head space above them.

Raw Pack

Pack raw green or wax beans tightly in clean, hot canning jars, leaving slight more than 1 inch of head space. Pour boiling water over the beans, leaving

1-inch head space. Wipe the jar rims clean and secure the canning lids.

Hot Pack

Blanch green or wax beans in boiling water for 5 minutes. Use a slotted spoon to transfer them to clean, hot canning jars. Loosely fill the jars, leaving slightly more than 1 inch of head space. Pour the still-hot blanching liquid over the beans, leaving 1 inch of head space. Wipe the jar rims clean and secure the canning lids.

Dial Gauge Canner

11 pounds; 20 minutes for pints, 25 for quarts. See the sidebar chart for high-altitude adjustments.

Weighted Gauge Canner

10 pounds; 20 minutes for pints, 25 for quarts. See the sidebar chart for high-altitude adjustments.

BEANS, FRESHLY SHELLED

Raw Pack

Loosely pack tender, freshly shelled beans into clean, hot canning jars, leaving slightly more than 1 inch of head space. Pour boiling water over the beans, leaving 1 inch of head space. Wipe the jar rims clean and secure the canning lids.

Hot Pack

Blanch tender, freshly shelled beans in boiling water for 3 minutes. Use a slotted spoon to transfer them to clean, hot canning jars. Loosely fill the jars, leaving slightly more than 1 inch of head space. Pour the still-hot blanching liquid over the beans, leaving 1 inch of head space. Wipe the jar rims clean and secure the canning lids.

Dial Gauge Canner

11 pounds; 40 minutes for pints, 50 for quarts. See the sidebar chart for high-altitude adjustments.

Weighted Gauge Canner:

10 pounds; 40 minutes for pints, 50 for quarts. See the sidebar chart for high-altitude adjustments.

BEETS

Scrub the beets clean and trim off all but an inch of the leaf stalks. Cook them in boiling water for 20 to 25 minutes. Remove the beets with a slotted spoon (reserve the cooking liquid). As soon as the beets are cool enough to handle, slip off the skins and slice off the stem and root ends. Leave very small beets whole. Cut larger beets into ½-inch-thick slices or cubes.

Hot Pack Only

Loosely fill the jars with the beets, leaving slightly more than 1 inch of head space. Bring the liquid the beets cooked in back to a boil and pour it over the beets in the jars, leaving 1 inch of head space. Wipe the jar rims clean and secure the canning lids.

Dial Gauge Canner

11 pounds; 30 minutes for pints, 35 for quarts. See the sidebar chart for high-altitude adjustments.

Weighted Gauge Canner

10 pounds; 30 minutes for pints, 35 for quarts. See the sidebar chart for high-altitude adjustments.

CARROTS

Slice off the stem ends and root tips of the carrots. Peel them. It's your choice whether to slice or dice them. Baby carrots may be left whole.

Raw Pack

Loosely pack the raw carrot pieces into clean, hot canning jars, leaving slightly more than 1 inch of head space. Pour boiling water over the carrots, leaving 1 inch of head space. Wipe the jar rims clean and secure the canning lids.

Hot Pack

Blanch the peeled carrot pieces in boiling water for 5 minutes. Use a slotted spoon to transfer them to clean, hot canning jars. Loosely fill the jars, leaving slightly more than 1 inch of head space. Pour the still-hot blanching liquid over the carrots, leaving 1 inch of head space. Wipe the jar rims clean and secure the canning lids.

Dial Gauge Canner

11 pounds; 25 minutes for pints, 30 for quarts. See the sidebar chart for high-altitude adjustments.

Weighted Gauge Canner

10 pounds; 25 minutes for pints, 30 for quarts. See the sidebar chart for high-altitude adjustments.

CORN

Raw Pack

Loosely pack raw corn kernels into clean, hot canning jars, leaving slightly more than 1 inch of head space. Pour boiling water over the corn, leaving 1 inch head space. Wipe the jar rims clean and secure the canning lids.

Hot Pack

Measure your raw corn kernels and put them into a pot. For each pint of corn, add ½ cup of water. Bring to a boil, reduce the heat, and simmer for 5 minutes. Ladle the corn and the cooking liquid into clean, hot canning jars. Leave 1 inch of head space. Wipe the jar rims clean and secure the canning lids.

Dial Gauge Canner

11 pounds; 55 minutes for pints, 85 for quarts. See the sidebar chart for high-altitude adjustments.

Weighted Gauge Canner

10 pounds; 55 minutes for pints, 85 for quarts. See the sidebar chart for high-altitude adjustments.

MUSHROOMS

Forget anything you might have heard about never washing mushrooms: Soak yours in clean water for 10 minutes, then rinse or scrub off any particles of dirt. Leave small mushrooms whole; cut larger mushrooms into slices or pieces not more than ½-inch thick.

Hot Pack Only

Blanch the cleaned and prepared mushrooms in boiling water for 5 minutes. Use a slotted spoon to transfer them to clean, hot canning jars. Loosely fill the jars, leaving slightly more than 1 inch of head space. Pour the still-hot blanching liquid over the mushrooms, leaving 1 inch head space. Wipe the jar rims clean and secure canning lids.

Dial Gauge Canner

11 pounds; half-pints and pints for 45 minutes. See the sidebar chart for high-altitude adjustments.

Weighted Gauge Canner

10 pounds; half-pints and pints for 45 minutes. See the sidebar chart for high-altitude adjustments.

OKRA

Although you have the option of slicing okra cross-wise into pieces for canning, you'll get much better results if you use small, firm, whole okra pods. Also, note that this is the only vegetable for which I do not recommend using the blanching liquid as the canning liquid.

Hot Pack Only

Blanch the okra in boiling water for 2 minutes. Use a slotted spoon to transfer them to clean, hot canning jars. Pack them somewhat tightly, leaving slightly more than 1 inch of head space. Pour fresh boiling water over the okra, leaving 1 inch head space. Wipe the jar rims clean and secure the canning lids.

Dial Gauge Canner

11 pounds; 25 minutes for pints, 40 for quarts. See the sidebar chart for high-altitude adjustments.

Weighted Gauge Canner

10 pounds; 25 minutes for pints, 40 for quarts. See the sidebar chart for high-altitude adjustments.

GREEN AND FRESHLY SHELLED PEAS

Raw Pack

Loosely pack tender, freshly shelled peas into clean, hot canning jars, leaving slightly more than 1 inch of head space. Pour boiling water over the peas, leaving 1 inch of head space. Wipe the jar rims clean and secure the canning lids.

Hot Pack

Blanch the freshly shelled peas in boiling water for 2 minutes. Use a slotted spoon to transfer them to clean, hot canning jars. Loosely fill the jars, leaving slightly more than 1 inch of head space. Pour the still-hot blanching liquid over the peas, leaving 1 inch of head space. Wipe the jar rims clean and secure the canning lids.

Dial Gauge Canner

11 pounds; 40 minutes for both pints and quarts. See the sidebar chart for high-altitude adjustments.

Weighted Gauge Canner

10 pounds; 40 minutes for both pints and quarts. See the sidebar chart for high-altitude adjustments.

SWEET PEPPERS

Remove the stems and seeds of sweet peppers. Cut into slices or pieces.

Although it is possible to pressure can hot chile peppers as described here, it is arguably the worst way to preserve them. Pickling, fermenting, dehydrating, or freezing are much better ways to preserve the fire and flavor of chiles.

Hot Pack Only

Blanch the peppers in boiling water for 3 minutes. Use a slotted spoon to transfer them to clean, hot canning jars. Loosely fill the jars, leaving slightly more than 1 inch of head space. Pour the still-hot blanching liquid over the peppers, leaving 1 inch of head space. Wipe the jar rims clean and secure the canning lids.

Dial Gauge Canner

11 pounds; half-pints or pints only, 35 minutes. See the sidebar chart for high-altitude adjustments.

Weighted Gauge Canner

10 pounds; half-pints or pints only, 35 minutes. See the sidebar chart for high-altitude adjustments.

PUMPKIN AND OTHER WINTER SQUASH

Canned pumpkin or winter squash is handy for making soups or adding to muffins and other baked goods. Unfortunately, it is not considered safe to home can puréed winter squash. So if you're going for that ready-to-use, already puréed pumpkin pie filling, opt for freezing rather than canning.

Cut the winter squash in half and scoop out the seeds. Cut the seeded halves into wedges, and then use a paring knife to remove the peels from the wedges. Cut the squash into approximately 1-inch chunks.

Hot Pack Only

Loosely fill clean, hot canning jars with the pumpkin or squash chunks, leaving slightly more than 1 inch of head space. Pour boiling water over the squash, leaving 1 inch of head space. Secure canning lids.

Dial Gauge Canner

11 pounds; 55 minutes for pints, 90 for quarts. See the sidebar chart for high-altitude adjustments.

Weighted Gauge Canner

10 pounds; 55 minutes for pints, 90 for quarts. See the sidebar chart for high-altitude adjustments.

Pressure Canning Soup Stocks

The canning instructions for vegetable, poultry, meat, and fish stocks are the same, assuming that we are talking about liquid only, no solid pieces of food. If there are chunks of meat or vegetables in what you want to preserve, then it's treated as a multi-ingredient soup, and the canning time will be longer (see the instructions for canning multi-ingredient recipes later in this chapter).

Dial Gauge Canner
11 pounds; 20 minutes for pints, 25 for quarts. See the sidebar chart for high-altitude adjustments.

Weighted Gauge Canner
10 pounds; 20 minutes for pints, 25 for quarts. See the sidebar chart for high-altitude adjustments.

Pressure Canning Meat (Beef, Pork, Lamb, Venison, and Game Meats)

STRIPS, CUBES, OR CHUNKS
Remove large bones and cut the meat into pieces. Soak game meats in a brine containing 1 tablespoon of salt per quart of water for 1 hour, then rinse before continuing.

Hot Pack
Cook the meat just until it's lightly browned on the outside but still quite rare on the inside. You may sauté it in a little fat, or steam, boil, or roast it.

Fill clean, hot canning jars with the pieces of meat, adding an optional ½ teaspoon of salt per pint if desired. Leave 1¼ inches of head space. Cover the meat with hot meat stock, tomato juice, and/or meat drippings, leaving 1 inch of head space. Wipe the rims of the jars clean and secure the canning lids.

Raw Pack

Add ½ teaspoon of optional salt per pint to the jars if desired. Fill the jars with raw pieces of meat, leaving 1 inch of head space. Do not add any liquid. Wipe the rims of the jars clean and secure the canning lids.

BOTH HOT AND RAW PACK:

Dial Gauge Canner

11 pounds; 75 minutes for pints, 90 for quarts. See the sidebar chart for high-altitude adjustments.

Weighted Gauge Canner

10 pounds; 75 minutes for pints, 90 for quarts. See the sidebar chart for high-altitude adjustments.

NO BONES, BOTH HOT AND RAW PACK:

Dial Gauge Canner

11 pounds; 75 minutes for pints, 90 for quarts. See the sidebar chart for high-altitude adjustments.

Weighted Gauge Canner

10 pounds; 75 minutes for pints, 90 for quarts. See the sidebar chart for high-altitude adjustments.

Ground or Chopped Meat

Brown the ground meat in a skillet over medium-high heat. You can shape patties out of the ground meat before browning, if you wish, but it isn't necessary. Venison benefits from the addition of a little pork fat during the cooking.

Hot Pack Only

Add an optional ½ teaspoon of salt per pint to clean, hot canning jars. Pour hot meat stock or tomato juice over the meat, leaving 1¼ inches of head space. Wipe the jar rims clean and secure the canning lids.

Dial Gauge Canner

11 pounds; 75 minutes for pints, 90 for quarts. See the sidebar chart for high-altitude adjustments.

Weighted Gauge Canner

10 pounds; 75 minutes for pints, 90 for quarts. See the sidebar chart for high-altitude adjustments.

Pressure Canning Poultry

Chill poultry in the refrigerator for at least 6 hours before canning it. Remove excess skin and fat. Cut the poultry into pieces that will fit into pint or quart canning jars, leaving the meat on or off the bone.

Hot Pack

Cook the poultry by steaming, boiling, or baking it (no frying) until it is approximately two-thirds cooked. Put the semi-cooked poultry into clean, hot canning jars, leaving 1½ inches of head space. Add optional ½ teaspoon salt per pint. Pour hot chicken or other poultry stock over the meat, leaving 1¼ inches of head space. Wipe the jar rims clean and secure the canning lids.

Raw Pack

Add an optional ½ teaspoon of salt per pint to clean canning jars. Fit in the poultry, leaving 1¼ inches of head space. Do not add any liquid. Wipe the jar rims clean and secure the canning lids.

PRESSURE CANNING POULTRY, BONE IN, BOTH HOT AND RAW PACK:

Dial Gauge Canner

11 pounds; 65 minutes for pints, 75 for quarts. See the sidebar chart for high-altitude adjustments.

Weighted Gauge Canner

10 pounds; 65 minutes for pints, 75 for quarts. See the sidebar chart for high-altitude adjustments.

PRESSURE CANNING POULTRY, NO BONES, BOTH HOT AND RAW PACK:

Dial Gauge Canner

11 pounds; 75 minutes for pints, 90 for quarts. See the sidebar chart for high-altitude adjustments.

Weighted Gauge Canner

10 pounds; 75 minutes for pints, 90 for quarts. See the sidebar chart for high-altitude adjustments.

Pressure Canning Rabbit

Make a brine of 1 tablespoon salt per quart of water, and soak the rabbit in it for 1 hour. Rinse. Remove excess skin and fat. Cut the rabbit into pieces that will fit into pint or quart canning jars, leaving the meat on or off the bone.

Hot Pack

Cook the rabbit by steaming, boiling, or baking it (no frying) until it is approximately two-thirds cooked. Put the semi-cooked rabbit into clean, hot canning jars, leaving 1½ inches of head space. Add an optional ½ teaspoon salt per pint. Pour hot rabbit, poultry, or veggie stock over the meat, leaving 1¼ inches of head space. Wipe the jar rims clean and secure the canning lids.

Raw Pack

Add an optional ½ teaspoon of salt per pint to clean canning jars. Fit in the rabbit meat, leaving 1¼ inches of head space. Do not add any liquid. Wipe the jar rims clean and secure the canning lids.

ON THE BONE, BOTH HOT AND RAW PACK:

Dial Gauge Canner

11 pounds; 65 minutes for pints, 75 for quarts. See the sidebar chart for high-altitude adjustments.

Weighted Gauge Canner

10 pounds; 65 minutes for pints, 75 for quarts. See the sidebar chart for high-altitude adjustments.

NO BONES, BOTH HOT AND RAW PACK:

Dial Gauge Canner

11 pounds; 75 minutes for pints, 90 for quarts. See the sidebar chart for high-altitude adjustments.

Weighted Gauge Canner

10 pounds; 75 minutes for pints, 90 for quarts. See the sidebar chart for high-altitude adjustments.

Pressure Canning Fish

Remove the scales, head, tail, fins, bones, and any entrails. Wash off any blood. Cut into 3- to 3½-inch pieces.

Raw Pack Only

Put the fish in clean pint canning jars with the skin side of each piece toward the outside of the jar. Leave 1 inch of head space. Wipe the rims of the jars clean and secure the canning lids.

Dial Gauge Canner

11 pounds; 100 minutes, pints only. See the sidebar chart for high-altitude adjustments.

Weighted Gauge Canner

10 pounds; 100 minutes, pints only. See the sidebar chart for high-altitude adjustments.

Crystals of magnesium ammonium phosphate sometimes form in home-canned fish, and as far as I know there is no way to prevent this. However, these crystals dissolve when heated in cooking, and are harmless.

Pressure Canning Clams and Other Shellfish

Keep the shellfish chilled until you are ready to can it. Scrub the shells clean. Steam for about 5 minutes until the shells open (discard any that do not open). Remove the meat, reserving the liquid in the shells. For oysters, instead of steaming, roast them for 5 minutes in a preheated 400°F oven.

Wash the shellfish meat with a brine made of 1 teaspoon salt per quart of water. Make a second brine with 2 tablespoons lemon juice or ½ teaspoon citric acid in a gallon of water. Bring this second brine to a boil. Add the shellfish meat and cook for 2 minutes. Drain in a colander.

Hot Pack Only

Loosely fill clean, hot canning jars with the prepared shellfish meat, leaving 1¼ inches head space. Cover the shellfish with the reserved juices and boiling-hot water, leaving 1 inch of head space. Wipe the rims of the jars clean and secure the canning lids.

Dial Gauge Canner

11 pounds; 60 minutes for half-pints, 70 minutes for pints. See the sidebar chart for high-altitude adjustments.

Weighted Gauge Canner

10 pounds; 60 minutes for half-pints, 70 minutes for pints. See the sidebar chart for high-altitude adjustments.

Canning Multi-Ingredient Recipes

When you want to can multi-ingredient recipes, such as pasta sauces, soups (other than simple, clear stocks), or the ratatouille recipe below, the pressure canning time is determined by the ingredient with the longest required processing time. For example, if I want to can a soup that includes carrots and chicken, carrots need a pressure canning time of just 25 minutes (for pints), but chicken requires a full 75 minutes. A soup including both those ingredients needs to be pressure canned for 75 minutes.

And although tomato sauce with added acid may be canned in a boiling water bath, if you add a lot of mushrooms, onions, and other low-acid ingredients to turn it into a pasta sauce, you need to pressure can it. The canning time will again be the one for the ingredient that needs the longest processing time.

HOW TO USE YOUR PRESSURE CANNER AS A BOILING WATER BATH

Your pressure canner can double as a boiling water bath for acidic foods. The instructions are a bit different from those for either pressure canning or regular boiling water bath canning.

Important: Remember that when you use this method, your pressure canner is functioning as a boiling water bath; it cannot be used in this way to pressure can low-acid foods. Only use this method with acidic ingredients that may be safely canned in a boiling water bath.

Fill your jars with the acidic food you are canning, leaving head space as always. Screw on the canning lids. Place the rack into your pressure canner, then put the jars on top of the rack, leaving space between them. Pour in hot water until it just covers the lids. This last step is different from both regular boiling water bath canning—in which the jars need to be covered by an inch or two of water—and pressure canning, in which the tops of the jars are not covered by water at all.

Secure the lid of the pressure canner by screwing or clamping it on. Leave the vent open and turn the heat on high. As soon as steam starts coming out of the vent forcefully, start timing your boiling water bath processing according to the recipe instructions. Leave the vent open the entire time. Remember that the processing time doesn't start when you turn on the heat, but only when steam starts coming out of the vent.

When the boiling water bath time is finished, turn off the heat and wait until there is no steam coming out at all before opening the canner and taking out the jars.

Ratatouille with Roasted Vegetables

PREP TIME: 10 minutes   COOKING TIME: 15 minutes   PRESSURE CANNING TIME: 30 minutes
YIELD: 3 to 4 pints

This is a colorful dish made with summer's peak season vegetables and herbs. If I'm making a summer menu that is going straight from garden to plate, I sometimes skip the roasting step. But if I'm going to pressure can the ratatouille, the roasting gives it a heartier taste that is perfect for warming up a winter meal. Serve ratatouille with good, crusty bread or over pasta or couscous.

INGREDIENTS

1 pound eggplant, stems removed and cut into 1-inch chunks

1 pound zucchini or other summer squash, stems removed and cut into 1-inch chunks

3 medium onions, peeled and thickly sliced

2 large red bell or sweet roasting peppers, cut into 1-inch squares

¼ cup plus 1 tablespoon extra-virgin olive oil, divided

3 large tomatoes

4 cloves garlic, minced

1 teaspoon fresh thyme leaves

¼ cup fresh basil leaves, shredded

Salt and pepper to taste

INSTRUCTIONS

1. Preheat the broiler of your oven.

2. In a large bowl, toss the eggplant, zucchini, onions, and sweet peppers with ¼ cup of the extra-virgin olive oil. Spread the vegetables on a baking sheet or two. Nestle in the tomatoes, whole.

3. Broil the vegetables for 5 to 10 minutes, until they are starting to show some browned spots but are not burned. Remove them from the broiler. Lift out and set aside the tomatoes to cool slightly apart from the other vegetables.

4. Heat the remaining 1 tablespoon of extra-virgin olive oil in a large pot over medium-low heat. Add the minced garlic and stir for 30 seconds. Add the thyme and the broiled vegetables (except for the tomatoes) to the pot. Cook, stirring occasionally, for 5 minutes.

5. While the other vegetables are cooking, remove the stems, most of the seed gel, and as much of the skins as peel off easily from the tomatoes. Coarsely chop the remaining pulp and stir the tomato into the other ingredients.

6. Remove the pot from the heat and stir in the shredded basil along with salt and pepper to taste.

7. Pack the ratatouille into clean, hot pint canning jars. Leave a ¾-inch head space. Wipe the rims of the jars clean and screw on the canning lids. Pressure can for 30 minutes at 10 pounds pressure (adjust the pressure if you live at a high altitude; see the sidebar in the this chapter).

CHAPTER SIX

Dehydrating

Dehydrating is almost certainly one of the original forms of food preservation. Not only is it an extremely easy task, but it also produces foods that are lightweight, take up much less space than their fresh counterparts, can be stored at room temperature, and keep pretty much forever. These attributes have made dehydrated foods mainstays of every civilization, and indeed contributed to the possibility of cultures moving from one land to another. From hunter-gatherer nomads to the crews of sailing ships to the modern hiker nibbling on trail mix, dried foods have always been a traveler's ally.

There are no bacteria, yeasts, or molds that can survive in the absence of moisture. This simple fact is what makes dried foods safe. Dehydrating food also slows down enzyme activity, although it does not eliminate it.

In arid climates such as Southern California or Mediterranean countries, dehydrating food can be as simple as putting it out in the sun under a screen that keeps out bugs. That's the original method of making sun-dried tomatoes, for example. But if you try that in a humid region like the eastern coast of North America, what you end up with is mold. For that reason, I've focused here on drying foods in either a dehydrator or an oven. The results are just as delicious as if they had, in fact, been dried in the sun.

Drying food in a dehydrator has three advantages over doing so in an oven:

- Dehydrator temperatures can be set as much as 50°F degrees lower than the lowest temperature in your oven.

- Built-in fans result in much better air circulation, which can shorten drying times by as much as half from using a conventional oven (convection ovens can match a dehydrator's speedier drying

times). This means that using your oven is almost always much less energy efficient than using a dehydrator.

- A dehydrator's stacking racks are much easier to work with than limited oven space paired with multiple baking sheets.

Obviously, I'm a fan of drying foods in a dehydrator rather than an oven. But for many years before I got a dehydrator, I did dry foods in my oven, and the results were good. If that's what you've got, use it.

Will dried foods taste like their formerly fresh selves once they're reconstituted in liquid? Never. But that's not a problem once you learn to enjoy them for their own unique flavors and textures. You don't expect a raisin to taste like a grape, do you? But raisins are just as good as the grapes they are made from—simply different.

Nutritionally, dried foods hold up well. They do lose vitamin C, but retain most of their vitamin A, all of their fiber, and most of their minerals and B vitamins. The minerals and B vitamins leach out into the soaking water when dried foods are rehydrated by steeping them in hot water. Don't throw that soaking water out! Not only does it contain some of the food's valuable nutrients, but it is loaded with flavor. I add the soaking water from rehydrating dried tomatoes to pasta sauces, and the mushroom flavor of risotto or any other dish is intensified if it includes the soaking water from dried, wild edible mushrooms.

How to Dry Fruit

Fruit dries beautifully, as anyone who has ever eaten a raisin or a dried apple knows. But to get the best results with home-dried fruit, there are a few best practices to follow.

Fruit that will be dried whole, such as grapes and cranberries, needs to be "checked." Checking fruit basically means cracking the skin. To do this, bring a pot of water to a boil and also prepare a large bowl of ice water. Put the whole fruits into the boiling water for 1 to 10 minutes, then drain them in a colander and immediately transfer to the ice water to stop the residual heat from continuing to cook the fruit. Drain again before drying the fruit.

Larger fruits such as apples dry best when peeled and sliced ⅛ to ¼ inch thick. It's not absolutely necessary to peel fruits before dehydrating them, but leaving the peels on lengthens the drying time and can result in an unpleasantly sharp texture at the edge of otherwise pleasingly chewy dried fruit.

Home-dried fruit can darken significantly as it dries. Commercially dried fruits with bright colors such as intensely orange-colored dried apricots are treated with sulfites before drying. It is possible to do this at home, but I don't recommend it. Most of us don't have ingredients such as sodium metabisulfite in our kitchen cabinets, for one thing, and many people's bodies are sensitive to sulfites and react to them with headaches, respiratory problems, and other symptoms.

Fortunately, there are other ways to pretreat fruit so that it keeps its color well. These all involve briefly soaking the fruit in acidulated water before dehydrating. Put just-sliced pieces of fruit immediately into the acidulated water and let them soak in it for 10 minutes before draining well and dehydrating. To make the acidulated water, use one of the following methods.

LEMON JUICE PRETREATMENT

Combine equal parts lemon juice and cold water.

CITRIC ACID PRETREATMENT

Dissolve 1 teaspoon of citric acid in 1 quart of cold water. Citric acid is sometimes available near canning supplies at supermarkets and hardware stores, or can be ordered online.

ASCORBIC ACID PRETREATMENT

Dissolve 1½ tablespoons of ascorbic acid crystals in 1 quart of cold water. Alternatively, crush vitamin C tablets and dissolve them in water (six 500ml tablets of vitamin C equals 1 teaspoon of ascorbic acid crystals, so you'll need 27 tablets for a quart of water). Ascorbic acid crystals are sometimes available at drugstores and supermarkets, or can be ordered online.

Once your fruit is "checked" and/or pretreated, spread it in a single layer on the trays of your dehydrator, or on racks set in baking sheets if you will be drying the fruit in your oven. Remember that the fruit will shrink a lot as it dries and can fall through a rack if its spaces are too big. This is not usually a problem with dehydrators, but can be when you are improvising a dehydrating rack in your oven. You can get around this problem by putting a finely meshed screen over the rack. Make sure none of the pieces of fruit are touching.

To dry in a dehydrator: Dry the fruit at 135 to 140°F.

To dry in an oven: Set the oven to its lowest temperature, which will usually be between 140 and 150°F. Put in the baking trays of fruit. Prop the door of the oven open with a dishtowel or the handle of a wooden spoon.

Whether you're working with a dehydrator or an oven, dry the fruit until it is leathery and no beads of moisture develop along the edges of a piece torn in half. Condition the fruit by letting it fully cool on the trays before transferring it to glass or stainless-steel jars or containers.

For the best-quality dried fruit, further condition it by filling the containers only two-thirds full of the just-dried fruit. Cover and shake the jar every day for one week. This will redistribute any residual moisture. If there are any signs of condensation on the insides of the container, the fruit is not fully dried and should be returned to the dehydrator or oven for a few more hours. After a week of conditioning the fruit, fully fill containers with it for storage (filling the jars only two-thirds full was just to make it easier to shake the fruit).

In addition to simply dehydrated fruits, there are a couple of slightly more involved methods that yield treats such as craisins and quince paste.

How to Dry Cranberries in a Dehydrator

Also called "craisins," dried cranberries are a wonderful snack and also great on salads, in baked goods, or with cereal or yogurt.

Dried Cranberries

Most commercially sold dried cranberries are sweetened. The instructions here include the sweetening step. You can skip sweetening your homemade craisins if you wish, but keep in mind that unsweetened cranberries can be extremely sour and astringent.

You can use this same method with other small, smooth-skinned berries such as blueberries and juneberries. Because they are naturally sweeter than cranberries, no need for the sweetening step with those other fruits.

INSTRUCTIONS

1. Prepare the cranberries by washing them and then "checking" them by pouring boiling water over them in a large bowl or pot. Let the berries soak in the scalding-hot water for 10 minutes. During that time most of them will pop (split open). Don't worry if there are a few duds that fail to pop—we'll take care of those later.

2. Drain the cranberries in a colander. While they are draining for several minutes, make a simple syrup by cooking 2 parts water and 1 part sugar over low heat. Stir until the sugar is completely dissolved.

3. Return the checked, drained cranberries to the bowl or pot they soaked in. Add the simple syrup and stir gently to coat the berries.

4. Cover the bottom of your dehydrator with a sheet of parchment paper or foil to catch any drips. Arrange the cranberries on the dehydrator trays, making sure that none are touching. While you are placing the cranberries on the trays, set aside any that did not pop during their soak in boiling hot water. After you've finished arranging the berries that did pop, go back to the ones that didn't and prick each with the tip of a paring knife before placing it on one of the dehydrator trays with the other cranberries.

5. Dry the cranberries at 150°F for the first half hour, then at 135°F for the rest of their time in the dehydrator. It will take between 8 and 14 hours for the berries to fully dry. You want a texture that is somewhat leathery or chewy, but there should be no visible beads of moisture on the break line when you tear one of the craisins in half. Start testing them for doneness after 8 hours (drying them overnight and then testing them when I get up in the morning is what I find easiest). Remember that the cranberries will feel a bit harder and drier after they have cooled, so turn the dehydrator off and let them cool for 20 to 30 minutes before testing them.

6. Condition the dried, cooled fruit by filling glass jars two-thirds full with the cranberries. Cover the jars and leave them at room temperature for 1 week. Shake the jars at least twice a day during the conditioning week. The conditioning step evenly redistributes any moisture the berries still contain. It also gives you a chance to confirm whether they are dried sufficiently for mold-free storage: If any condensation appears on the inner sides of the jars during conditioning, return the cranberries to the dehydrator or oven at 135°F for a few hours more.

7. After the conditioning week, combine the cranberries so that the jars are completely full. (Filling them only two-thirds full was just so that you could shake the fruit around during the conditioning phase.)

Fruit Leather

Also called roll-ups, fruit leathers are a healthy, portable snack. Kids love them (as do grown-ups), and because they are lightweight and take up little space, they are perfect for lunch boxes or to take on a hike.

INSTRUCTIONS

1. Start with fruit that is very ripe. Peel and core fruits such as pears and apples. Remove the pits from other types of fruit such as apricots and peaches (you could also peel these for a smoother fruit leather, but it's not essential).

2. Chop the fruit into 1-inch pieces. Put an inch of water in the bottom of a double boiler (you can improvise a double boiler by setting a large heatproof mixing bowl over a water-containing pot). Put the fruit into the top of the double boiler. Cover, bring the water to a boil, and cook 15 to 20 minutes until the fruit is soft and registers 160°F on a thermom-

eter. It is necessary to heat the fruit to this internal temperature to kill off potential pathogens before making fruit leather with it.

3. Let the fruit cool for 5 minutes (take it off of the bottom of the double boiler). Purée it in a blender or food processor before proceeding with either the dehydrator or the oven method below.

IN A DEHYDRATOR

4. Line your dehydrator's trays with nonstick dehydrator sheets, plastic wrap, or parchment paper.

HOW TO MAKE FRUIT LEATHERS FROM CANNED FRUIT

This is a great way to use up the remnants of last year's canned fruit when the new harvest season gets under way.

Fruit that is already puréed, such as applesauce or pear butter, can be used straight out of the jar. Simply proceed to step 4 of the dehydrator or the oven method for making fruit leathers.

If you are working with larger pieces such as canned peach halves, let them drain in a colander for a few minutes. If the fruit was canned in a sugar syrup, rinse it with water before draining. Purée the drained fruit in a blender or food processor. Continue from step 4 of one of the fruit leather methods above.

5. Put 1 cup of fruit purée in the center of each tray. Use a spatula to spread it out until it is 1/8 inch thick.

6. Dehydrate at 140°F for 4 to 10 hours. The huge variation in time there is because of the difference in density of various fruit purees. Start checking after 4 hours. The fruit leather is done when it is translucent, barely sticky to the touch, and peels easily away from the nonstick sheet.

7. Let the fruit leather cool to room temperature before rolling it up in plastic wrap or waxed or parchment paper.

IN THE OVEN

4. Line a baking sheet with plastic wrap or parchment paper. Tuck the edges under the baking sheet. Alternatively, lightly grease it with vegetable oil.

5. Two cups of fruit puree is plenty for a 12 x 17-inch baking tray. Use a spatula to spread the puree 1/8 inch thick.

6. Turn the oven to its lowest setting, somewhere between 140 and 150°F. Dry the fruit leather for 4 to 10 hours. The huge variation in time there is because of the difference in density of various fruit purees. Start checking after 4 hours. The fruit leather is done when it is translucent, barely sticky to the touch, and peels easily away from the nonstick sheet.

7. Let the fruit leather cool to room temperature before rolling it up in plastic wrap or waxed or parchment paper.

Quince Paste

PREP TIME: 10 minutes   COOKING TIME: 3 hours   DRAINING TIME: 2 hours
DRYING TIME: 8–12 hours   CHILLING TIME: 4 hours   YIELD: Approximately 1 pound

---

Called membrillo in Spain, this paste takes the homely, pale quinces that are in season in late fall and transforms them into a glistening holiday food gift that has a deep rosy color and delightfully tangy taste. Solid enough to be thinly sliced, quince paste can also be used as a spread. It is often served with a salty, aged cheese such as manchego, but is also excellent as a breakfast treat with cream cheese and bagels or toast.

INGREDIENTS

3½ pounds quinces (that's about 4 large quince fruits)

Water

2 pounds sugar

INSTRUCTIONS

1. Wash and peel the quinces, saving the peels. Cut the quinces in half and then cut out the cores, adding these to the reserved peels. Chop the peeled and cored quince fruit into 1- to 2-inch pieces.

2. Tie the quince peels and cores up in cheesecloth, butter muslin, or a clean cloth produce bag. Don't tie them up too tightly—you want liquid to be able

to reach all the surfaces of the peels and cores. We're after the high quantity of pectin that they contain.

3. Put the pieces of quince and the bundle of cores and peels into a large pot. Add enough water to cover them by about an inch. Bring the ingredients to a boil over high heat, then reduce the heat and simmer them for 1 to 1½ hours until the fruit is soft and mushy.

4. Use tongs to remove the bundle of peels and cores. Drain the remaining quince fruit either in a very finely meshed strainer or through a double layer of cheesecloth set in a colander. You might want to put a big bowl or pot underneath to catch the liquid that drains out: you can use it to make an exquisitely aromatic, jewel-colored quince jelly using the general jelly directions in the Sweet Preserves chapter. Let the quince drain for a full 2 hours.

5. Purée the cooked and strained quince mash. The easiest way to do this is in a food processor, but you could also run the mash through a food mill, or use the back of a spoon to press it through a colander or strainer.

6. Weigh the quince puree. Add it and an equal amount of sugar to a large pot. If you don't have a kitchen scale, you can measure rather than weigh the quince and sugar, but weighing gives better results.

7. Cook the quince purée and sugar over low heat until thick. This will take approximately 1½ hours. At first you'll need to stir constantly to dissolve the sugar. Once the sugar has dissolved, it's okay to just stir about once every 5 minutes until the quince really starts to thicken up near the end of its cooking time. You'll know it is done when the paste sticks to a wooden spoon. Also, if you drag a wooden spoon across the bottom of the pot and it leaves a clear trail that does not fill in right away with the quince, then it is ready. Be sure to stir constantly as the quince paste approaches this stage so that it does not stick to the bottom of the pot and burn.

   During its cooking time, the quince that started out the color of pale apple flesh will turn a deep blush color.

8. Lightly grease a 9-inch baking dish with vegetable oil. While it is still hot, spread the quince paste evenly in the pan. It should be approximately 1½ inches thick. Wait until the paste has completely cooled in the pan before proceeding with the next step.

9. To dry the *membrillo* in a dehydrator, remove all but the bottom tray from the dehydrator. Place the baking dish with the quince paste on the bottom tray and set the dehydrator to 125°F.

   To dry the *membrillo* in your oven, put the dish of quince paste into the oven, and set the oven to 125°F. If your oven doesn't go that low (many don't), put it on its lowest setting and prop the door open with a dishtowel or the handle of a wooden spoon.

   Dry the quince for 8 hours or overnight, after which its surface should be glossy and not sticky to the touch.

10. Put the baking dish of quince paste in the refrigerator and leave it there, uncovered, for 4 hours.

11. Run a table knife around the edges of the quince paste. Put a plate on top and then invert it onto the plate. You can either wrap the whole square of membrillo in plastic wrap or waxed paper, or you can first cut it into logs that are about the size of a stick of butter. Once wrapped, quince paste will keep in the refrigerator or cold storage for at least 3 months.

How to Dry Vegetables

Dried vegetables aren't just useful to have on hand for winter stews. You can also add them to casseroles, and even baked goods such as zucchini bread. Dried carrots, onions, and celery work just as well as fresh as aromatics when you make soup stocks. And in soup recipes besides stocks, I find dried vegetables are excellent in puréed soups (the texture is a bit off, though, when they are left in whole pieces in most soups). Like all dehydrated foods, dried vegetables have the advantages of being compact, lightweight, and shelf-stable, which means they are easy to travel with and you don't need electrical power to store them.

The drying times for vegetables can range from as little as 4 hours to as much as 24 hours, depending on how thick the pieces are and whether they are dried with good air circulation in a dehydrator or convection oven, or in a conventional oven.

Whether you are drying vegetables in a dehydrator or in your oven, it is important that air can circulate freely around the pieces of food while they are drying. This means that you want to spread the vegetables out in single layers and without the pieces touching.

Slice or chop vegetables into pieces approximately ¼ inch thick before dehydrating them. For most vegetables, 135°F is a good average temperature. Before you dry them, you need to blanch many vegetables by briefly immersing them in boiling water. This step destroys enzymes that would otherwise survive the dehydration process. The result is that the vegetables keep their colors and flavors much better. For example, if you dehydrate celery without blanching it first the result is the color of straw. But blanched, celery keeps its bright green hue for well past a year in storage.

To blanch vegetables, bring a large pot of water to a boil. Chop the washed vegetables into pieces between ⅛ and ½ inch thick. Drop the vegetables into the boiling water and leave them there for the amount of time specified in the following chart. Drain them in a colander, then immediately transfer them to a large bowl of ice water or run them under very cold water until they are completely chilled. Drain again before dehydrating.

How to Dry Tomatoes

Dried tomatoes are such a wonderful ingredient in their own right that it's worth drying some just for the unique flavor. Home-dried tomatoes taste just as great as the "sun-dried" ones you buy at the store, but without the high cost. And tomatoes do not need to be blanched first, which makes them one of the easiest foods to dehydrate.

Any kind of tomato may be dried, but for the best results choose small paste tomatoes such as the Principe Borghese variety. Cut the tomatoes into halves, strips, or slices, depending on how large they are. The pieces should ideally be no thicker than ¼ inch. Squish out and discard the seedy gel; this step is optional, but results in a vastly briefer drying time and a tastier end product.

Arrange the prepared tomato pieces skin-side down on dehydrator trays or on baking sheets lined

with racks or parchment paper. Make sure that none of the pieces are touching.

IN A DEHYDRATOR

Set the dehydrator to 135°F and dry the tomatoes for 8 to 14 hours, depending on the thickness of the pieces.

IN AN OVEN

Set your oven to its lowest temperature, which will typically be between 140 and 150°F. Place the baking sheets of tomatoes in the oven and dry for 6 to 12 hours, depending on the thickness of the tomatoes. If your oven heats unevenly, turn the baking sheets around at least once during the drying time.

The tomatoes will be either leathery or brittle when they are fully dried. A piece cut in half should show no moisture along the break line. If in doubt, err on the side of brittle (you'll be reconstituting them to a softer texture in hot water eventually, so don't worry if they seem crunchier than their store-bought counterparts).

When they come out of the dehydrator or oven, let the tomatoes cool at room temperature before transferring them to tightly sealed jars or containers.

To reconstitute dried tomatoes, put them in a heatproof bowl and pour boiling water over them. Let them soak for 15 minutes before draining. Don't throw out that soaking liquid! It is full of the flavor of the tomatoes. Add it to soups, sauces, or pasta cooking water.

HOW LONG TO BLANCH BEFORE DEHYDRATING

VEGETABLE	TIME
Asparagus	4–5 minutes
Beans, green and wax	4 minutes
Beets	10 minutes
Brussels sprouts	4 minutes
Cabbage	5–6 minutes
Carrots	4 minutes
Cauliflower	4–5 minutes
Celery	4 minutes
Chile peppers	Don't blanch
Corn	4–6 minutes
Eggplant*	4 minutes

VEGETABLE	TIME
Leafy greens	4 minutes
Okra	4 minutes
Onions*	4 minutes
Parsnips	4 minutes
Peas	4 minutes
Peppers, sweet	4 minutes
Potatoes	7 minutes
Summer squash (includes zucchini)	4 minutes
Winter squash (includes pumpkin)	6 minutes

*optional; can be dried without blanching, but color may darken

Oven Method Kale Chips the Quick Way

PREP TIME: 10 minutes   BAKING TIME: 10–15 minutes   YIELD: Approximately 1 quart

---

These crunchy, savory snacks are so delicious they are almost addictive, and yet they are so much healthier than fried chips.

It's crazy how much kale chips cost at the store. Make your own and not only will you save money, but you won't be adding all that plastic packaging to the landfill.

INGREDIENTS

1 large bunch kale (any variety, but lacinato, also called dinosaur kale, seems to hold its crunch longer than others)

1 tablespoon extra-virgin olive oil

¾ teaspoon salt

¾ teaspoon nutritional yeast (optional, but adds an interesting cheesy flavor)

¼ teaspoon cayenne powder (optional)

INSTRUCTIONS

1. Wash the kale. Dry the leaves in a salad spinner or by rolling them up in a dish towel.

2. Strip any tough midribs out of the kale leaves by holding the stem end in one hand while you gently pull down along the leafstalk from stem to tip with your other hand. Tear the kale into pieces just slightly larger than you want your chips to be (they don't shrink as much while drying as other vegetables do).

4. Put the kale pieces into a large mixing bowl. Toss them with the extra-virgin olive oil until all are coated with the oil. Your clean hands are the best tools for this job.

5. Line a baking sheet with parchment paper. Spread the kale leaves on the lined baking sheet, taking care not to crowd the leaves. It's okay if they over-lap a tiny bit, but they should be in a single layer, not piled on top of one another. Use more than one baking sheet if necessary. Sprinkle the kale with the salt, and the nutritional yeast and cayenne if you're using these.

6. Bake for 10 to 15 minutes until the kale pieces are crisp but not burned.

7. Take the tray(s) out of the oven and let the kale chips cool completely before transferring them to paper bags or tightly sealed storage containers. For longer storage, if you have a vacuum sealer you can seal them in plastic, but regular plastic bags don't work well for kale chips.

8. If your kale chips lose their crunch in storage, you can restore it by spreading them out on a baking sheet and baking them in a preheated 300°F oven for 5 minutes. They will get crispy again as they cool.

Dehydrator Method Kale Chips

PREP TIME: 10 minutes   DEHYDRATING TIME: 4–5 hours   YIELD: Approximately 1 quart

---

If you have a dehydrator, definitely use it instead of your oven to make kale chips. It will take hours instead of minutes, but the results will have better color and there's no possibility of burning them as there is with the oven-dried kind.

INGREDIENTS

1 large bunch kale (any variety, but lacinato, also called dinosaur kale, seems to hold its crunch longer than others)

1 tablespoon extra-virgin olive oil

¾ teaspoon salt

¾ teaspoon nutritional yeast (optional, but adds an interesting cheesy flavor)

¼ teaspoon cayenne powder (optional)

INSTRUCTIONS

1. Wash the kale. Dry the leaves in a salad spinner or by rolling them up in a dish towel.

2. Strip any tough midribs out of the kale leaves by holding the stem end in one hand while you gently pull down along the leafstalk from stem to tip with your other hand. Tear the kale into pieces just slightly larger than you want your chips to be (they don't shrink as much while drying as other vegetables do).

4. Put the kale pieces into a large mixing bowl. Toss them with the extra-virgin olive oil until all are coated with the oil. Your clean hands are the best tools for this job.

5. Spread the olive-oil-coated kale pieces out on the dehydrator trays. As with the oven-dried method, take care not to crowd the leaves. It's okay if they overlap a tiny bit, but they should be in a single layer, not piled on top of one another. Once each tray is filled, sprinkle the kale with the salt, and the nutritional yeast and cayenne (if you're using these), before putting the tray into the dehydrator.

6. Set the dehydrator's temperature to 145°F and dry the kale for 1 hour. Reduce the dehydrator's temperature to 115°F and dry the kale for an additional 3 to 4 hours until the pieces are crispy-dry.

7. Turn off the dehydrator and let the kale chips cool completely before transferring them to paper bags or tightly sealed storage containers. For longer storage, if you have a vacuum sealer you can seal them in plastic, but regular plastic bags don't work well for kale chips.

8. If your kale chips lose their crunch in storage, you can restore their crispness by spreading them out on a baking sheet and baking them in a preheated 300°F oven for 5 minutes. They will get crunchy again as they cool.

Dehydrator Method Kale Chips the Raw Food Way

PREP TIME: 10 minutes   DEHYDRATING TIME: 4–5 hours   YIELD: Approximately 1 quart

Only this method qualifies these chips as "raw." In order to be considered raw, a food has to be dried at temperatures below 118°F; warmer than that, and the enzymes in the food are killed off.

INGREDIENTS

1 large bunch kale (any variety, but lacinato, also called dinosaur kale, seems to hold its crunch longer than others)

1 tablespoon extra-virgin olive oil

¾ teaspoon salt

¾ teaspoon nutritional yeast (optional, but adds an interesting cheesy flavor)

¼ teaspoon cayenne powder (optional)

INSTRUCTIONS

Follow the instructions for oven drying kale chips on page 154, but just through step 4. Then:

5. Spread the olive-oil-coated kale pieces out on the dehydrator trays. As with the oven-dried method, take care not to crowd the leaves. It's okay if they overlap a tiny bit, but they should be in a single layer, not piled on top of one another. Once each tray is filled, sprinkle the kale with the salt, and the nutritional yeast and cayenne (if you're using these), before putting the tray into the dehydrator.

6. Set the dehydrator's temperature to between 110 and 115°F and dry the kale for 8 to 12 hours until the pieces are crispy-dry.

7. Turn off the dehydrator and let the kale chips cool completely before transferring them to paper bags or tightly sealed storage containers. For longer storage, if you have a vacuum sealer you can seal them in plastic, but regular plastic bags don't work well for kale chips.

8. If your kale chips lose their crunch in storage, you can restore their crispness while keeping their raw food status by putting them back into a dehydrator set to between 110 and 115°F for 1 hour.

Dried Green Beans

It's not a requirement that you blanch green beans before you air-dry them, but it does make a big difference in the color of the final product. If blanched first, they will still be green when you eventually rehydrate them. If not, they darken, turning almost black. They are still safe to eat in that case, but not as appealing on the plate.

You can also dry yellow wax beans, as well as thinly sliced sweet peppers with this method.

INSTRUCTIONS

1. Wash the green beans. Snap or cut off the stem ends.

2. To blanch the beans, if you choose to do so, bring a large pot of water to a boil. Add the green beans and boil them for 3 minutes. Drain them in a colander and then quickly transfer them to a large bowl of cold water to prevent the residual heat from continuing to cook them. Leave them in the cold water for 3 minutes, then drain them again.

3. Thread a large needle such as an embroidery needle with kitchen string or unflavored, unwaxed dental floss. Pierce a green bean with the needle about 1 inch down from either end. Secure that first bean by drawing the string through until there

is a 2-inch tail left. Tie the tail to the main thread, securing a knot there.

4. Thread the next green bean onto the string, leaving ½ inch of space between it and the first bean. Continue threading beans onto the string, piercing them about 1 inch down from either end and leaving that ½ inch of space between them. When you have used up almost all of the string, remove the needle and tie the end of the thread to the main thread (around the last bean).

5. Hang the string of green beans in a dry place with good air circulation. In about a week the beans will have shrunk considerably and their texture will be somewhere between leathery and brittle.

6. Transfer the "leather britches" to clean, dry jars or food storage containers and cover them tightly.

7. To use them, first give them a rinse in cool water. Then put them in a bowl and pour boiling water over them. Let them soak until they soften (but remember that they still are not cooked). Simmer them in water or stock until tender and then add them to casseroles and soups, or go with the traditional and very tasty recipe of frying the cooked shoestring beans up with a little bacon.

How to Air-Dry Green Beans, or "Leather Britches"

Air-dried green beans were staple fare back in pioneer times, when they were usually called "leather britches" or "shoestring beans." The whimsical names come from the fact that once dried, green beans do shrivel up and look like strips of leather or maybe like old shoestrings. I know that description doesn't make them sound like the sexiest ingredient in the pantry. But the technique of making them is easy, they keep indefinitely, and the flavor and texture of the rehydrated, cooked beans is excellent (though totally unlike fresh green beans).

How to Dry Herbs

Whether you are preserving some of your garden's aromatic abundance, or simply don't want to waste the rest of that bunch of sage you bought and only used a few leaves of, drying is one of the best ways to preserve most (but not all) herbs. Home-dried herbs have richer colors, scents, and tastes than even the best store brands. It is the essential oils in most herbs that gives them both their aroma and their taste—a scentless culinary herb is going to be flavorless as well. Because these oils are very volatile and evaporate easily, the best results come from drying the herbs quickly but with minimal exposure to light and heat. I find the best way to do this is to simply dry them at room temperature, with a brief finishing in a very low oven only if necessary. It is possible to dry herbs in a dehydrator, but I find the results less flavorful.

Leafy herbs can be dried by using a rubber band to hold 8 to 10 sprigs together. Don't get all artsy and tie them up with raffia or yarn: The stems will shrink as they dry and fall out of such quaint ties. Stick to rubber bands. Hang the bundles of herbs somewhere away from direct heat or light. After a week, the herbs should be dry enough to crumble easily off the stems when crushed. In very humid environments, you may need to finish them in the oven. To do this, put herbs

that have already dried for a week in your oven on its lowest temperature setting for no longer than 5 minutes. Let them cool at room temperature for an additional 5 minutes before transferring them to jars. Do not leave them out any longer than this or they will reabsorb moisture from the air.

Non-leafy herbs including flowers, roots, seeds, and barks can be dried in paper or cloth bags, or in a single layer between two finely meshed window screens laid on top of each other horizontally. They can be finished with the same quick oven treatment described above.

There are a few leafy herbs that lose so much of their flavor when dried that they should be preserved by other methods. Herbs that do not dry well include chives, parsley, basil, chervil, and cilantro (coriander leaves). These herbs can be preserved as salts, butters, oils, or vinegars.

Dried leafy herbs and flowers will keep for 1 year, after which they lose most of their flavor. Roots, barks, and seeds will keep for considerably longer if left whole or in large pieces, but also only for a year if they are already finely ground when stored.

How to Dry Mushrooms

Drying is by far the best way to preserve most mushrooms. Mushrooms that dry well include supermarket button mushrooms, but also morels, maitake, shiitake, porcini, and other wild (or cultivated) edible mushrooms. Mushrooms are the exception to the rule that dehydrated foods are entirely different ingredients from their fresh counterparts: Once reconstituted,

dried mushrooms can be used interchangeably with fresh in any cooked recipe.

Clean the mushrooms and slice them into pieces between ¼ and ½ inch thick. Morels are best dried whole or in halves (you can thread whole morels on a string and hang them from the racks in your oven to dry them).

To dry mushrooms in a dehydrator, arrange the pieces in single layers on the dehydrator trays so that none of the pieces overlap. Dry at 110°F until crispy-dry, which will take between 4 and 8 hours depending on how thickly you sliced the mushrooms.

To dry mushrooms in an oven, preheat the oven to its lowest setting, which will usually be between

140 and 150°F. Arrange the mushroom pieces in a single layer on a baking sheet so that none of the pieces overlap. Dry in the oven for 1 hour. Turn the pieces over and dry them for another hour.

Whether you dried your mushrooms in a dehydrator or oven, let them cool off at room temperature for 10 minutes before transferring them to tightly sealed containers. This conditioning period is important, and you won't know until it's over whether your mushrooms are fully crispy-dry.

How to Dry Meats (Including Poultry and Fish)

Most dried meat products are a blend of salt curing, smoking, and dehydrating … as you'll see in the next chapter. But it is possible to dry meat in a dehydrator without the curing or smoking, as the following simple but delicious recipe demonstrates.

Jerky from Ground Turkey

PREP TIME: 5 minutes   MARINATING TIME: 1 hour, 15 minutes   DEHYDRATING TIME: 4–6 hours
OVEN FINISHING 10 minutes   YIELD: 4 large pieces jerky

Use a combination of dark and light turkey meat for the best results with this recipe. You can also use hamburger instead of turkey meat for an easy version of beef jerky.

INGREDIENTS

1 pound ground turkey (I recommend a 50–50 mix of light and dark meat, if possible)

Juice and zest of 1 lemon

2 tablespoons grated onion

1 tablespoon soy sauce or tamari

1 tablespoon Worcestershire sauce

1 tablespoon sugar or 2 teaspoons honey

1 tablespoon extra-virgin olive oil

2 teaspoons sweet paprika

1 clove garlic, grated (tip: peeling and then freezing the garlic first makes it easier to grate)

1 teaspoon salt

1 teaspoon ground black pepper

½ teaspoon liquid smoke (optional)

⅛ teaspoon ground cayenne pepper (optional)

INSTRUCTIONS

1. Keep the ground turkey meat chilled in the refrigerator until you are ready to use it. Meanwhile, mix all of the other ingredients together and let them sit for 15 minutes while the flavors marry.

2. Add the ground turkey to the other ingredients and use your clean hands to combine them well. Put the seasoned turkey into the refrigerator for 1 hour.

3. Lay out a sheet of parchment paper on a work surface. Scoop out approximately a quarter of the jerky mixture and put it onto the parchment paper. You can either pat it down by hand, or put a second sheet of parchment paper on top of the meat and roll it out with a rolling pin. Either way, it should be between ⅛ and ¼ inch thick.

4. Remove the top sheet, if you used one. Put one of the dehydrator trays on top upside down and flip the whole thing over, transferring the jerky to the tray. Remove the remaining sheet of parchment paper.

5. Patch any holes by patting in bits of raw jerky mixture.

6. Repeat with the remaining turkey jerky mixture until you have spread it out on four dehydrator trays.

7. Dry for 4 to 6 hours at 155°F. Check on your jerky after 4 hours. You want it to be fully dried but still chewy, not brittle. If this stage seems tricky to identify, don't worry: The next step ensures your turkey jerky is sufficiently dried for food safety.

8. When you think your jerky is sufficiently dried, preheat your oven to 275°F. Transfer the jerky to baking trays and finish it off in the preheated oven for 10 minutes.

CHAPTER SEVEN

Salting and Smoking

I've paired salting and smoking in this chapter because almost all *preserved* smoked foods start out with a salt cure, or a salt-and-sugar cure. I'm making a distinction here between smoking food just to flavor and cook it versus actually preserving it. Although smoking the food does partially dehydrate it and kill off surface bacteria, the salt-curing part of the process is much more essential from a food safety standpoint than the smoking part. Food may be safely preserved with salting alone; food that is smoked without being cured may be flavorful, but it is usually not safely preserved.

The first two recipes below demonstrate different methods of using salt to preserve food without smoking it. The recipes after that show how to combine salt curing with smoking.

Dry Salting

Pack fresh food in so much salt that it covers every bit of the food's surface: That's dry salting. Almost any solid food can be preserved this way, from green beans to mushrooms to fish. It is one of the classic ways to cure olives, capers, *bacalau* (salt cod), and more.

When straight-up salt is used in this way, not only does it create an environment that is so alkaline harmful bacteria cannot survive in it, but more important it dehydrates any living cells. This either kills the potentially harmful organisms, or renders them inactive.

MAKING HERB SALTS

This is a great way to preserve fresh herbs that don't dry well, such as cilantro, rosemary, and chives. It couldn't be simpler.

INGREDIENTS
4 parts very finely minced herbs (a food
processor comes in handy here)
1 part kosher or medium-fine-grain sea salt

That's it. Stir well to combine and then pack the herb salt in clean glass containers. Cover tightly and store in a cool, dark place indefinitely. Use herb salts on roasted root vegetables, meats, or popcorn; mixed into dips, salad dressings, or marinades; and anywhere else you're inspired to.

Moroccan-Style Preserved Lemons

PREP TIME: 10 minutes   YIELD: 1 pint

Preserved lemons are an essential ingredient in Moroccan tagines and other North African dishes. They make a lovely gift, especially if paired with a recipe.

INGREDIENTS

¼ cup kosher or sea salt

1 tablespoon sugar or 2 teaspoons light honey

4–5 organically grown lemons, quartered lengthwise

2 whole cloves

1 cinnamon stick

Juice of 3–4 additional lemons

INSTRUCTIONS

1. Combine the salt with the sugar.

2. Pack the quartered lemon pieces into a clean glass pint jar, pressing down on each layer as you add them. Sprinkle the lemon pieces with the salt-and-sugar mixture as you add them. Press the two cloves down in between the lemon pieces. Slide the cinnamon stick in between the lemons and the side of the jar.

3. Add the additional lemon juice, pressing down gently on the lemon pieces to remove any air bubbles, until the pieces are completely submerged in liquid. Screw on the lid.

4. Leave out at room temperature for 1 week. Shake the jar daily to help dissolve the salt and sugar. Open the jar after each time you've shaken it and push the lemon pieces back under the brine if they have floated up out of it.

5. Transfer to the refrigerator or other cool, dark place. Preserved lemons are ready to use 2 weeks after you transfer them to the refrigerator. They keep indefinitely, but their quality is at its peak during the first 6 months.

Salt Fish

PREP TIME: 5 minutes (if starting with filleted fish)   SALTING TIME: 2 days
DRYING TIME: 1 to 2 weeks

Although cod is the most famous fish for this preservation method, I encourage you to use whichever lightly flavored, flaky, white fish you can get that is sustainably caught. Alas, as of this writing cod is overfished to the point of endangerment in many places. A quick search online will update you on which fish you can use with a clear conscience.

Once you've made salted fish, you've got the makings of the French *brandade* (or in Spain, *brandada*), Portuguese stew, and many other iconic dishes. And because the salt fish is soaked for at least a day before using, it actually isn't at all salty in the final recipes.

INGREDIENTS

Cod, haddock, flounder, or other mild, flaky fish fillets
Kosher or medium-grain sea salt

INSTRUCTIONS

1. Rinse the fish and dry it with a clean dishcloth or with paper towels. Spread a layer of salt at least ½ inch thick in a container. Lay pieces of fish on top so that none of them are touching. Cover the pieces of fish with another thick layer of salt.

Repeat the alternating salt and fish layers until you've buried all of the fish in salt (be sure to finish with a ½-inch layer of salt on top).

2. Put the salted fish into the refrigerator, uncovered, and leave it for 2 days.

3. Brush as much of the salt off the fish as you can (don't worry if you don't remove every speck). Wrap the fish in cheesecloth. Set it on a rack over a plate or tray and put it back into the refrigerator for another week or two.

4. Remove the cheesecloth. Store the salted fish in a closed container in the refrigerator or a cold cellar.

5. To use salt fish, first soak it for at least 24 hours, changing the water at least twice during that time. Two days of soaking and a couple more changes of water is even better.

Curing

Curing begins by rubbing meat or fish with a mixture of salt, sometimes sugar, sometimes spices, and sometimes curing salts containing sodium nitrite and/or sodium nitrate. During the curing process, the food releases liquid and becomes much more solid than it was initially. Surface bacteria are eliminated by the alkaline cure.

Smoking

There are two kinds of smoking, one used primarily for imparting flavor to the food, and one that does that and also helps to preserve the food by dehydrating rather than cooking it:

Hot smoking is done at temperatures at or above 150°F, typically between 150 and 200°F. It flavors and cooks the food, but doesn't really preserve it. Hot smoking is usually the finishing touch after a salt (or salt-and-sugar) cure has already done most of the food preservation work.

Cold smoking is done at temperatures just below 100°F. It dehydrates the food as well as giving it that umami smoke taste. The catch is that it's very difficult to maintain a controlled temperature of around 90°F for hours unless you invest in a smoker with controls.

ABOUT DIFFERENT TYPES OF SMOKERS

Smokers can range from an improvised, vented container set over a small fire piled with damp wood chips, to sophisticated machines costing thousands of dollars, to many variations in between. Which kind you need depends on whether you are mostly interested in cold smoking or hot smoking food.

To simply add flavor to food, including already cured meats such as bacon, a very simple smoker is fine because you will be hot smoking. But if you want

to make something that must be cold smoked, then you need a smoker that at the very least has a temperature gauge and a way to adjust and maintain a temperature around 90°F with minimal fluctuation.

Most smokers burn charcoal, but there are some gas models.

For most purposes, a charcoal-burning smoker with an accurate temperature gauge, adjustable vents, and a means of buffering the heat from the burning coals (such a fitted water bowl in between the fire and the food) will be sufficient. These simply designed smokers require attention, but are moderately priced. By opening and closing the vents and by adjusting the amount of water in the buffer bowl, you can do a fairly good job of controlling the temperature.

ABOUT DRYING AFTER CURING AND BEFORE SMOKING

When cured meat is air-dried, it develops a tacky surface called a pellicle. In the smoker, smoke adheres to the pellicle. That's why you'll get a tastier smoked bacon, for example, if you let it dry overnight after curing and before smoking.

Pancetta

Pancetta starts out with a sweet-and-salty cure like bacon, but much more highly seasoned with herbs. Then, instead of being roasted or smoked, pancetta is air-dried for several weeks.

INGREDIENTS

2–3 pound slab pork belly

2 cloves garlic, peeled and minced, or
   1 teaspoon garlic powder

1 teaspoon pink curing salt #1
   (optional but recommended)

2 tablespoons kosher or medium-fine-grain sea salt

1½ tablespoons ground black pepper, divided

10 juniper berries, crushed

2 bay leaves, broken into pieces

½ teaspoon ground nutmeg

Leaves from 2–3 sprigs fresh thyme

INSTRUCTIONS

1. Rinse the pork belly under cold water, then pat it dry with a clean dishcloth or paper towels.

2. Unlike the bacon-making process, for pancetta you're going to remove the rind-like skin from the pork belly before you cure it. Do this by laying out the pork belly skin-side up, and sawing with a sharp knife back and forth horizontally just under the skin.

3. Combine all of the other ingredients, except for 1 tablespoon of the ground black pepper, in a large bowl or on a large plate. Rub them into the pork belly. Make sure to get the seasoned curing mixture into every nook and cranny of the pork.

4. Put the pork belly, along with any curing mixture that isn't already rubbed into it, into a nonreactive container (glass, food-grade plastic, or stainless steel). Cover the container and refrigerate it for 1 week. Once a day, flip the bag over, or flip the pork belly over inside the container.

5. After a week, the pancetta should feel firm even at the thickest part of the meat. If it is still very soft, cure it in the refrigerator for another day or two. Once the pork belly is fully cured and firm, rinse it well under cold water and dry it thoroughly with a clean dishcloth or paper towels.

6. Lay the pork belly out meat-side up (fat layer underneath). Rub the remaining ground black pepper into the meat side. Roll the pork belly up into a tight cylinder (you can't roll it too tightly) and secure the roll with kitchen twine, butcher's string, or unflavored and unwaxed dental floss.

7. Hang the pancetta to air-dry in a humid, cool place like your unheated basement. Ideally the temperature should be between 50 and 60°F and the humidity close to 60 percent, but you've got some wiggle room with that. Definitely hang it away from direct light or heat. If the humidity is low and the pancetta starts to dry out, put it on a rack set over a dish in the refrigerator with a plastic bag or big container set loosely upside down over the rack. Let it air-cure for 2 weeks.

8. After it has been dried, wrap your pancetta tightly in plastic wrap or butcher's paper. It will keep in the refrigerator for up to 1 month, and in the freezer for at least 4 months. To eat, cut your pancetta into thin slices or slivers and fry it as you would bacon.

Bacon

There are so many reasons to make bacon at home rather than cooking with store-bought!

For starters, the taste is usually far superior and you have choice about how to slice it. For super-thin slices that cook into the crispy breakfast strips Americans are familiar with, freeze the bacon to make it easier to slice that thin. Or you can choose to turn your bacon into lardons, the slightly chewy, small strips or dice of cooked bacon the French use to flavor hearty dishes such as coq au vin.

You've noticed by now that it is important to me to be able to choose the healthy quality of the ingredients that go into my food. By making my own bacon rather than purchasing it, I can opt to include curing salt (nitrite) or not. And I can and will always choose to use pork belly from a pastured, organically fed animal that was not injected with antibiotics or hormones.

Most bacon sold in the United States is first sugar-and-salt cured, then smoked. But many other countries skip the smoking. The final smoking step is a question of flavor rather than preservation with homemade bacon, and it is your choice whether to do it. Smoked or unsmoked, all bacon is gently cooked at a low temperature after its salt curing, but requires additional cooking before serving..

INGREDIENTS

2–3 pounds pork belly (choose a pork belly that is approximately half fat and half lean meat)

½ cup brown sugar or ¼ cup granulated sugar plus ¼ cup molasses or maple syrup

½ cup kosher or other medium-fine, non-iodized salt

1 teaspoon freshly ground black pepper

¾ teaspoon curing salt (optional)

GEAR

Meat thermometer

Smoker (optional: See step 6 for how to get that smoked bacon flavor with and without a smoker)

INSTRUCTIONS

1. Rinse the pork belly under cold water, then pat it dry with a clean dishcloth or paper towels. One side of the pork belly will have a skin like a thick rind; leave that on for now.

2. Combine the sugar (or sugar plus molasses or maple syrup), salt, and pepper in a large bowl. Add the pork belly and massage the cure into it with your scrupulously clean hands.

3. Put the pork belly plus any curing mixture not already sticking to it into a sealable food container or bag. Seal and store it in the refrigerator for 7 to 14 days. Turn the pork belly over every other day to redistribute the curing mixture. The bacon is cured when it has a much firmer consistency than it started out with and has no soft spots.

4. Rinse the bacon under cold water and pat it dry. For unsmoked bacon, place a rack in a baking dish and put the bacon on the rack. Roast the bacon in a 200°F oven until the internal temperature reaches 150°F. This will take about 2 hours.

5. Slice off the pork belly skin now, while the bacon is still hot. Once it has cooled to room temperature, store the bacon, well wrapped, in the refrigerator for up to 3 weeks, or in the freezer for up to 1 year.

6. For smoked bacon, there are two ways to go:

    If you have a smoker, instead of step 4 (above), first let the bacon dry by setting it in the refrigerator overnight, uncovered. The next day, hot smoke the cured pork belly at around 200°F until it reaches an internal temperature of 150°F. Use hickory or a fruit tree wood such as apple or pear for the best flavor.

    If you don't have a smoker, you can "cheat" and get that smoked flavor by using liquid smoke. Simply roast the bacon in the oven as for unsmoked bacon, above. When the internal temperature of the bacon reaches 150°F, take it out of the oven and immediately baste it on all sides with liquid smoke.

Smoked Trout

PREP TIME: 5 minutes if starting with cleaned fish   BRINING TIME: 24–48 hours   DRYING TIME: 30 minutes
COLD SMOKING TIME: 3–4 hours   HOT SMOKING TIME: 4–12 hours

This method that combines both cold and hot smoking works with other medium-small fish (salmon, whitefish, grayling) as well as trout. The result is a delicious ingredient that can be enjoyed as is or used in recipes. Try smoked trout blended with cream cheese for a delicious dip, or combine it with pan-fried potatoes and chopped mustard greens for a wonderful breakfast hash.

Although you can make tasty smoked trout by simply hot smoking it, keep in mind that the result will be simply flavored and cooked, not preserved. To use this combination of cold and hot smoking that preserves the fish for longer keeping, you will need a smoker with an accurate temperature gauge and allows you to adjust the temperature with some precision. Keep in mind that although this method will extend the keeping time of your fish by weeks or months, it will not preserve the fish indefinitely.

INGREDIENTS

½- to 1-inch-thick trout fillets or halves *or* 1 whole fish (scales and viscera removed)

Brine

2 quarts water

½ cup kosher or medium-fine-grain sea salt

¼ cup sugar *or* 2 tablespoons honey

½ teaspoon pink curing salt #1 (optional)

2 crumbled or torn bay leaves

1 whole clove

4 whole allspice berries

½ teaspoon dried sage

GEAR

Meat thermometer

Smoker

INSTRUCTIONS

1. Combine the brine ingredients, stirring to dissolve the salt and sugar or honey. Add the fish and use a plate with a jar full of water or other weight on top of it to keep the fish submerged in the brine. Let the fish soak in the brine in the refrigerator for as little as 2 hours or as much as 24.

2. Drain the fish. Rinse it under cold water and then pat it dry with either a clean dish towel or paper towels. Lay the fish out on a rack set over a dish or tray and let it dry at room temperature for approximately 30 minutes. As the fish dries, a shiny, tacky layer called a pellicle will form. The pellicle seals in juices that keep the fish tender and also gives the smoke something to adhere to, which results in richer smoke flavor in the final product.

3. While the fish is brining and drying, get your smoker ready. If you are using commercial charcoal plus soaked wood chips, start the wood chips soaking in water. Use only hardwoods such as apple, pear, birch, or maple wood. Also only use hardwoods if you are making your own hot coals from a wood fire. Do not use spruce, pine, or other conifers, as they can give the fish an off taste.

Whether you are starting with commercial charcoal or creating your own from a wood fire, keep some hardwood chips soaking in water throughout the process to add as needed. These will be providing the smoke (and flavor) while the coals are providing the heat.

4. Cold smoke the fish for 2 to 3 hours at between 90 and 100°F. Note that on the hottest days of summer in some places the ambient air temperature may be greater than this: Smoking trout is a cool-weather project. Add wet wood chips to the coals as needed to keep a consistent amount of smoke wafting toward the fish. Open the vents as necessary to maintain the temperature.

5. Separately from the smoker, start another wood fire or get some charcoal burning. A charcoal chimney is useful for this. Add hot coals to the smoker and bring the temperature up to 225°F. Insert a digital thermometer into the thickest part of the fish. Maintain the 225°F temperature as closely as you can until the internal temperature of the fish reaches 180°F. This will usually take about 3 to 4 hours, but if you've got an especially big fish and are smoking it whole, it could take as long as 12 hours. During this time, continue to add soaked hardwood chips to the coals to keep that smoke encircling the fish.

6. Once the internal temperature of the fish reaches 180°F, maintain it there for an additional 30 minutes in the smoker.

7. Remove the fish from the smoker. Let it cool. Once it's completely cooled to at least room temperature (or colder if you're undertaking this project outdoors on a chilly day), wrap the fish tightly in foil or butcher's paper; you can also vacuum seal it. It will keep, refrigerated, for up to 1 month and in the freezer for at least 3 months.

CHAPTER EIGHT

Freezing

Even people who don't think they can cook, never mind practice food preservation, probably have some food stashed in their freezer. Freezing is one of the easiest forms of food preservation. Often it is the preferred method for preserving certain ingredients. Most berries, many vegetables, and all types of meat, poultry, and fish hold up admirably in the freezer. And for convenience, nothing beats pulling some soup or another already cooked recipe out of the freezer and simply heating and serving.

HOW FREEZING PRESERVES FOOD SAFELY

Freezing does not actually sterilize food the way exposure to extremely hot temperatures can. Instead, it renders bacteria inert. It also drastically slows the rate of chemical reactions that would otherwise cause the food to spoil.

There are, however, a few downsides to freezing food. Unless you're simply putting food outside in the chilliest part of winter, it requires electricity. Storage space is limited to the size of your freezer. And if it's improperly wrapped or kept for too long, your food can develop freezer burn or simply decline in quality.

To prevent freezer burn and minimize quality decline, you need to package the food well. In all cases, this means minimizing the amount of air the surface of the food is in contact with. So, for example, if you're putting some blanched and chopped kale into a freezer bag, be sure to press the bag as flat as possible before sealing it. It is possible to buy equipment to vacuum seal food, which definitely extends the length of time you can store it in the freezer. But wrapping food and minimizing air exposure works well, too. An exception to the "minimize air exposure" guideline is when freezing liquid foods such as soup stocks and stews. If you freeze these in solid-sided containers rather than freezer bags, you need to leave an inch of air space above the food because the water in the food will expand when it freezes.

Some parts of your freezer are colder than others. As is true with your refrigerator, the shelves on the door harbor the warmest temperatures. Only foods with low water content such as nuts should be stored there long-term. Other foods will develop freezer burn if stored on the door of the freezer for more than a couple of weeks.

For energy efficiency, keep your freezer packed full. Not only does this use less electricity, but in the event of a power outage, the food will stay frozen longer in a packed-full freezer. This is the opposite of what you want for energy-efficient refrigerator use, by the way: There should be enough space between food items in your refrigerator for air to circulate freely (see the Cold Storage chapter for more details on this).

Do not refreeze frozen food that has already been completely thawed. Because water in the food expands and contracts as it is frozen and thawed, repeating the freeze–thaw pattern causes cell membranes to rupture and large ice crystals to form in the food. This destroys its texture, and can also expose the food to bacterial degradation during the thawed phase. However, if you've taken something out of the freezer and then changed your mind about using it, you can still return it to the freezer so long as it's still at least partially frozen.

How Long Can I Keep Food in the Freezer?

Here are the maximum lengths of time you should store different foods in your freezer. Your food will still be safe to eat if frozen longer, but its nutritional value will decline and its quality will nose-dive.

BAKED GOODS INCLUDING BREADS

Bread . . . . 3 months
Cookie and pie dough . . . . 6 months
Muffins and quick breads . . . . . . 2 months
Pancakes and waffles . . . . 1 month

BEANS AND GRAINS

Soaked (but not cooked) . . . . 4 months
Cooked . . . . 6 months
Rice and other grains, cooked . . . . 4 months

DAIRY

Although all types of dairy products including milk and cheese may be safely frozen, these are the only ones that survive freezing without a radical change in their texture and/or flavor.

Butter . . . . 9 months
Ice cream . . . . 2 months
Sorbet . . . . 2 weeks

FRUIT

Old-fashioned instructions often called for tossing fruit in sugar or sugar syrup before freezing it. This is unnecessary for the safe preservation of the fruit, and you'll have a healthier, fresher-tasting product if you skip it.

Apples . . . . 4 months
Apricots . . . . 6 months
Bananas . . . . 8 months
Berries . . . . 6 months
Cherries . . . . 6 months
Cranberries . . . . 1 year
Peaches . . . . 4 months
Fruit juice . . . . 1 year

LEFTOVERS

Casseroles and lasagna . . . . 4 months
Soups, stews, chili, and chowders . 6 months

PESTOS AND OILS

Herbal oils . . . . 8 months

Pesto (without cheese) . . . . 8 months
Pesto (with cheese) . . . . 3 months

MEAT
Bacon and pancetta . . . . 3 months
Chops. . . . . 6 months
Ground meats. . . . . 4 months
Organ meats . . . . 4 months
Roasts. . . . . .1 year
Sausage . . . . 3 months
Steaks. . . . . 8 months

MUSHROOMS
Mushrooms with a fairly dry texture such as supermarket button mushrooms or some wild ones such as maitake freeze well raw. Ones that have a higher moisture content, such as oyster mushrooms, are better sautéed before they are frozen.
Cooked mushrooms. . . . . .1 year
Raw mushrooms . . . . 8 months

NUTS
Shelled . . . . .2 years

POULTRY
These freezer storage times apply to all types of poultry, including chicken, turkey, and duck.
Whole bird. . . . . .1 year
Raw pieces. . . . . 9 months
Giblets . . . . 4 months
Cooked Poultry Meat . . . . 4 months

SEAFOOD
Fatty fish (including bluefish, salmon, and mackerel). . . . . 3 months

Lean and white fish
(cod, flounder, haddock, sole) . . . . 6 months
Crab, cooked . . . . 2 months
Crab, raw. . . . . 3 months
Crayfish, raw . . . . 4 months
Lobster, cooked. . . . . 2 months
Lobster, raw . . . . 3 months
Shellfish, cooked . . . . 3 months
Shellfish, raw . . . . 4 months
Squid, calamari, octopus, raw . . . . 4 months

SOUP STOCKS
Meat, poultry and vegetable stocks 6 months
Fish stock . . . . 4 months

VEGETABLES
Some vegetables such as leafy greens need to be blanched before they are frozen. Blanching times and instructions are given elsewhere in this chapter.
Asparagus. . . . . .1 year
Beet roots . . . . .1 year
Peppers (sweet, bell, and chile) . . . 4 months
Broccoli. . . . . .1 year
Carrots . . . . .1 year
Cauliflower . . . . .1 year
Celery. . . . . .1 year
Corn. . . . . 8 months
Green and wax beans . . . . .1 year
Leafy greens. . . . . 8 months
Okra. . . . . 8 months
Peas . . . . 8 months
Tomatoes . . . . 4 months
Winter squash including pumpkin, cooked 1 year
Summer squash including zucchini . 8 months

Why You Need to Blanch Some Foods Before Freezing, How to Do It, and When to Bother

Ever stick some sprigs of raw basil into a ziplock bag and shove it into your freezer? When you took it out weeks or months later, it thawed into a blackened, slimy mess, right? If you'd blanched the basil before freezing, it would have kept its emerald-green color and bright aroma and flavor. Here's why.

Although the temperatures in your freezer are too low for harmful bacteria to survive, they do not destroy the enzymes whose job it is to decay organic matter. In other words, that raw basil did, in fact, continue to slowly decompose even though it was frozen. Blanching, which is simply a very brief treatment in boiling water or steam, kills off those enzymes.

To blanch foods for freezing, bring water to a boil in a large pot or underneath a steamer basket. Drop in clean vegetables or herbs for just the amount of time specified (the water in the pot or steamer must be at a full boil before you start timing). Once the time is up, immediately drain the blanched food in a colander and then either transfer it to a bowl of ice water or run it under very cold water. This last step stops residual heat from continuing to cook the food. Squeeze out or drain off as much water as possible before transferring the blanched veggies or herbs to freezer containers and freezing.

I find that sweet and chile peppers, as well as onions, corn, and tomatoes may be frozen without blanching with good results. Most root vegetables, especially potatoes, do not freeze well even if they are blanched first (and yes, that includes carrots, despite the numerous commercial frozen vegetable combos that contain them). Here are some ingredients that blanch and freeze well:

BLANCHING TIMES FOR FREEZING VEGETABLES AND HERBS

Artichoke Hearts. . . . . 6 minutes
Asparagus . . . . 2–4 minutes
Beans, green or wax . . . . 3 minutes
Broccoli (in 1-inch pieces
or florets). . . . . 2 minutes
Brussels sprouts . . . . 3–5 minutes
Cauliflower
(in 1-inch pieces or florets). . . . . 3 minutes
Kohlrabi (in 1-inch cubes) . . . . . . 1 minute
Leafy greens (including chard,
collards, kale, spinach, etc.) . . . .1–2 minutes
Leafy herbs, fresh . . . . 20–30 seconds
Okra. . . . . 2–3 minutes

Peas (in the pod) . . . . 2–3 minutes

Peas (shelled, loose) . . . . 1.5 minutes

Squash (summer, chayote,
zucchini) . . . . 3 minutes

The Best Way to Freeze Berries and Chopped or Sliced Ingredients

If you dump a bunch of berries or chopped fruits or vegetables into a container and freeze them, what you get is a solid brick of frozen food that you probably only need a fraction of for the recipe you're making. Instead, do a double freeze. First, spread out the berries or chopped vegetables in a single layer on cookie or baking sheets and freeze them for 1 to 2 hours. Then transfer the frozen bits of food to freezer containers and return them to the freezer. The berries or veggie pieces will stay loose so that you can take out just what you need.

When you are chopping vegetables for this double-freeze method, keep their end use in mind. Do you tend to use sweet peppers more often chopped into dice than slices? Then that's how you should freeze them.

The Best Way to Freeze Meat, Poultry, and Seafood

When you freeze meats, including poultry and seafood, the goal is to prevent exposing the surface of the food to both air and moisture. It is possible to do

WHAT ABOUT FREEZING EGGS?

Eggs will keep, refrigerated for a month, so freezing them is usually unnecessary. However, if you find yourself with a surplus, it is possible to freeze beaten eggs for future use in sauces or baked goods (you'll never get a good omelet from frozen eggs). You can separate the yolks from the whites and freeze them apart from each other, or leave them combined. Either way, whisk until frothy and add 1 tablespoon of sugar or ½ teaspoon of salt per cup of beaten eggs. This addition helps to prevent the graininess that plagues frozen eggs. Freeze the egg mixture in ice cube trays, then transfer to freezer bags or containers. Two cubes equals 1 egg; ¼ cup equals 2 egg yolks, or 1 egg white.

this by tightly wrapping the meat in plastic wrap and then again in aluminum foil. You can vacuum seal the food in plastic if you have a vacuum sealer (see Useful Resources). You can get away with plastic freezer bags, which are thicker than regular plastic food storage bags, if you press out as much air as possible. But many people are trying to minimize the use of plastic nowadays, and wrapping meat directly in foil can give the food an off, metallic taste.

The best solution is to wrap the meat tightly in butcher's paper. Butcher's paper is waxed on one side (that's the side that should be touching the meat), and is available from office and craft supply stores (I know, it's bizarre to see butcher's paper right next to your kids' school supplies, but there it is). Once you've wrapped the meat in the butcher's paper, tape it shut with masking tape. Now wrap the package

again, this time with foil. Label with another piece of masking tape on which you've written the contents and the date. You can reuse the foil wrapping over and over, but the paper wrapping is single-use only (you can, however, recycle it in most places).

How to Make and Freeze Basil Oil (or Other Herbal Oil)

This is really a combination of two food preservation methods: preserving in fat and freezing. Basil isn't the only herb this method works great with: You can use it with cilantro (coriander leaves) and any other tender leafy herb that doesn't dry well.

Bring a large pot of water to a boil. Get a large bowl of ice water ready if your tap water isn't extremely cold.

Briefly swirl a bunch of basil in the boiling water (and I do mean briefly, not more than 30 seconds; 20 is plenty). Immediately transfer the blanched basil to the ice water, or run cold tap water over it to cancel out the residual heat (you want the herb to be blanched, not cooked). This blanching-then-chilling step ensures that your basil oil will keep its lovely bright green color once thawed (skip it and you'll have blackened muck).

Squeeze the basil hard to remove as much water as possible, or roll it up in a dishcloth and then squeeze that. Strip the leaves off of the stems and put them into a blender or food processor. Add an approximately equal amount by volume of good-quality extra-virgin olive oil. Puree the basil and oil.

soups, as a dipping sauce for bread, or of course on pasta. Or you can use it as a base for pesto by simply adding garlic, Parmesan cheese, and pine nuts or walnuts.

If you make a big batch of pesto intending to eat some right away and freeze the rest, do bother with the blanching-and-freezing step so that your pesto keeps its light emerald color even after it has been frozen and thawed. It's best to leave out the garlic and add some just before serving because it can develop a bitter taste when frozen.

How to Blanch and Freeze Leafy Greens

This is by far my favorite way to preserve leafy green vegetables, including kale, chard, spinach, and collards. The texture is infinitely better than that of canned greens, and they retain much more of their nutritional value (sorry, Popeye).

You definitely need to blanch leafy greens before freezing them, but it only takes a minute or two.

Bring a large pot of water to a boil. If your cold tap water is not very cold, get a bowl of ice water ready.

Wash the greens and remove any tough midribs. Stir them into the boiling water and let them blanch for 1 to 2 minutes.

Drain the blanched greens in a colander, then immediately run cold water over them or transfer them to the bowl of ice water. Once the greens are completely cooled, drain them again. Squeeze out as much liquid as possible (squeeze hard).

There are two handy ways to freeze the basil oil once you've made it. One is to pour it into freezer bags and seal. Spread the basil oil out in the bag horizontally: It should be no more than ⅛ inch thick. Once it's frozen, you'll have a sort of basil oil pancake. Break off just what you need when you want to use some.

The other method is to spoon the basil oil into the chambers of an ice cube tray. Once frozen, transfer the cubes of basil oil to freezer bags or containers.

Use basil oil as is—it's wonderful on top of bean

Chop the blanched greens and transfer them to freezer bags or containers. Label and freeze.

Notice that I didn't chop the greens before blanching them, but after. If you chop them before, the little pieces stick to the sides of the pot and the colander and are just a pain to work with. Chopping after blanching makes the process (including clean-up) much easier.

Two Ways to Freeze Fresh Ginger

Have you ever thrown out fresh ginger because you didn't get to it before it started to shrivel up or mold? Never again! Here are two easy ways to preserve fresh ginger.

The simplest way is to cut the ginger rhizome into 1-inch chunks. Use the double-freeze method to prevent the chunks from sticking together: Freeze in a single layer on a cookie sheet or plate first, then transfer the pieces to freezer bags or containers. You don't need to peel the ginger first. In fact, it will be easier to peel and chop or grate after it is frozen.

The second way is to peel and mince or grate the fresh ginger before freezing. This takes a little extra work up front, but the result is ready to go straight into recipes without even needing to thaw first. If you opt for this method, spread a thin layer of the minced or grated ginger in a freezer bag before sealing and freezing. The double-freeze method doesn't work as well here.

The Best Way to Freeze Cooked Leftovers

Soup, casserole, chili ... many cooked dishes freeze beautifully and reward you with an easy-to-prepare meal later on (need I mention that the huge frozen food industry is largely based on this?). It is well worth making a little extra when you cook and stashing what you can't eat right away in the freezer for the future. But there are a couple of tips that will make freezing leftovers even more practical.

Because water expands when it freezes, your leftovers will, too. When filling freezer containers with more liquid foods such as soup, always leave an inch of head space between the food and the lid for the food to expand into as it freezes.

Think about portions when you're deciding which size freezer containers to use for your leftovers. If you live alone, freeze individual portions, for example. Or just enough for a family of four, or whatever is appropriate for your current situation. What you want to avoid is refreezing food because you thawed a bigger quantity than you could eat. Refreezing always results in major quality decline.

The Only Way to Preserve Avocado

Freezing is the only way I know of to preserve avocado (if I'm wrong and there's another way, please let me know!). Once frozen, avocado purée is ready to use in guacamole, breakfast smoothies, or salad dressings. If you luck into a sale on avocados, are headed on a trip before you had a chance to eat the one on your counter, or are blessed to have a prolific avocado tree, this is what to do with the ones you won't getting around to eating fresh.

Only freeze fully ripe avocados: They won't get any better than they are when you put them into the freezer. Leave unripe avocados out at room temperature until they ripen to the point that the flesh gives easily when you press the avocado with your thumb.

Once the avocado(s) you want to freeze is fully soft and ripe, cut it in half lengthwise and separate the halves. Whack a large knife into the center of the avocado pit (watch your fingers) and give the knife a twist. The pit will come right out.

Scoop out the avocado flesh and put it into a food processor or blender (the food processor will work better). Add 1 tablespoon of lemon or lime juice per 8 ounces of avocado (that's about 1 medium avocado's

worth). The citrus juice prevents discoloration. Purée the avocado and citrus juice until smooth. Do not leave chunks even if you like your guacamole chunky: It won't freeze as well (you can always augment with some fresh avocado pieces before serving).

Put the avocado purée into freezer bags or containers. Leave 1 inch of head space if you're using containers, because the avocado will expand as it freezes.

CHAPTER NINE

Cold Storage

Whether it's a traditional root cellar dug like a Hobbit-hole straight into a hillside, or the crisper drawers of a technologically state-of-the-art new refrigerator, cold storage is the food preservation method that stores fresh, raw vegetables and fruits at temperatures that are cool but never freezing.

The Four Essentials of Successful Cold Storage

To understand how cold storage works, you need to remember that even after a pear is picked or a carrot dug out of the ground, it is still alive. Respiration continues (yes, plants "breathe") even after plant foods are harvested, and there are still living enzymes present in them. Some of those enzymes are meant to decompose the food as part of nature's own composting system. Cool temperatures slow down respiration and enzymatic activity, delaying (although not permanently eliminating) spoilage.

Cold air absorbs less moisture than warm air, so cold storage also helps keep fresh food from drying out. Nonetheless, you need to give humidity some thought when using cold storage.

Root cellars should have 80 to 95 percent humidity (more about that in the Root Cellaring section below). Inside refrigerators, the air tends to be extremely dry despite the cool temperatures. That is why fresh fruits and vegetables should be loosely wrapped even when stored in the produce crisper drawers, which have higher humidity than elsewhere in the refrigerator. Ever toss a bunch of carrots into the crisper without first putting them into a bag or container? Remember how they were already starting to shrivel up in a matter of days? That's a good example of why high humidity is an important part of cold storage. Optimal humidity levels can be achieved by maintaining moisture levels in the air and/or by preventing moisture loss through evaporation by wrapping the food.

In addition to cool temperatures and humidity, there are two other factors essential to successful food cold storage: air circulation and darkness.

Air circulation prevents condensation on the surface of the food. This is especially important for any cold-stored foods that are not individually wrapped. Although high humidity is important for successful cold storage, in a root cellar without good air circulation moisture sitting on the surface of the food could cause rot. Root cellars require ventilation systems that allow cool nighttime air in while releasing the warm, moist air that builds up in them. These systems also vent the ethylene emitted by some fruits (a natural gas that causes ripening and eventually spoilage). Ethylene is the secret behind the trick of putting unripe fruit in a bag with an apple or banana to ripen them, by the way: The apple or banana emits ethylene that ripens the other fruits.

Good cold storage is also light controlled, meaning that the food is stored primarily in darkness. The exceptions are those occasions when you want to take something out of your cold storage area and need enough light to see by. The light in your refrigerator takes care of this by remaining off unless the door is opened. In a walk-in root cellar, you should provide a light that is near the entrance, making it easy to turn off and on. For smaller cold storage situations, a flashlight may be sufficient. At no time should the food be exposed to numerous hours of daylight. The reason for this is that some vegetables, including potatoes and onions, will start to sprout if exposed to light, so it is important to store them in the dark as much as possible.

So those are the four crucial factors for using cold storage to extend the edibility of fresh produce for many weeks or even months: cool temperatures, high humidity, good air circulation, and darkness.

Let's start with the cold storage system that almost everyone has in their home, and how to get the most out of it.

Where to Store What in Your Refrigerator

In many homes, the refrigerator has replaced the cool cellar where past generations stored perishables. But are you making the most of yours? Inside your refrigerator there are microclimates, each better suited for some foods than others. For example, the temperatures of the fridge door are warmer than on the main shelves, and the lower shelves on both the door and main area are warmer than the upper shelves.

Wait, isn't that backward? Heat rises, so shouldn't the upper shelves be warmer than the lower? You would think so, but in most refrigerators the cold air is emitted from the top down, so the upper shelves are the coldest.

Here's the info on what goes where.

FRIDGE DOOR

This is the warmest part of your refrigerator, but even it has temperature variations. The upper compartments are cooler than the lower, and are where you should store butter and eggs. Egg compartments often have a plastic cover that insulates the eggs from the circulation of cold air. If yours doesn't, you could create the same effect by storing your eggs in a covered container set on one of the upper shelves of your refrigerator door. Condiments such as salad dressings, ketchup, jam, and pickles do okay stored on the fridge door. Your milk does not!

TOP SHELF

Store milk, yogurt, and other dairy products except for cheese on the top shelf of the main body of your refrigerator, if possible. Fruit juices should also be stored there, as well as leftovers.

MIDDLE SHELF(S)

Store meat, ripe fruit, and any produce that won't fit into the crisper drawers here.

BOTTOM SHELF

Store cheeses and cold cuts here unless your refrigerator has a midsection drawer for them. Vacuum-sealed foods, including store-bought products still in their original packing, should be stored here.

CRISPER DRAWERS

These are where your fresh vegetables should go. But remember that the air inside a refrigerator is very dry, if less so in the crisper drawers. Always store your produce in containers or plastic bags, not just loose and exposed.

Best Refrigerator Practices

Unlike your freezer, which is most energy efficient when packed full of food, your refrigerator functions best when it is just moderately full. You want air to circulate easily between food items.

Do not leave your refrigerator door open for more than 30 seconds if you can help it. Yes, that means no staring for too long at the contents of your fridge while you debate what to snack on. Why? Well, when you open the door of your fridge you let in huge amounts of warm air while cold air simultaneously spews out from the lower part of the fridge. After just 30 seconds with the door open, the temperature within the refrigerator can be as much as 15°F degrees higher than it was with the door shut. And it can then take as long as 15 minutes for the inside of the refrigerator to chill back to its original temperatures.

Refrigerator Pickle Recipes

I already shared a dill cucumber refrigerator recipe in the Vinegar Pickling chapter. Here is another classic refrigerator pickle recipe.

One of the great things about refrigerator pickles is that they are ready to eat in as little as 1 to 4 days (they'll keep for months, though). The disadvantage is that they do need to be stored at very cold temperatures. So if the power goes out and you don't have a comparably cold cellar, they won't keep long.

This same disadvantage means that they aren't as easy to give as gifts—whereas canned pickles can sit, gift-wrapped, at room temperature until the recipient opens them, refrigerator pickles can't.

Nonetheless, I am a big fan of refrigerator pickles. Because they rely on a combination of acidic brine and cold storage, you can use less vinegar in them than you have to with other recipes. What this means to you, the eater, is a much lighter flavor. Also, the lack of canning time usually means a crisper texture.

Giardinieri: Mixed Italian Antipasto Garden Pickle

PREP TIME: 15 minutes   COOKING TIME: 5 minutes   YIELD: 1 quart; recipe can be multiplied

---

The beauty of this recipe is that it uses up a little of this and a little of that, perfect for people with small gardens who may not have bushels of any one vegetable at any given time. The vegetables included here are traditional for this style of pickle, but the truth is you can use whatever is coming in from your garden (or in season at the farmers' market).

The extra-virgin olive oil on top of the *giardinieri* is there more as a flavoring than a preserving factor. The pickles pass through the oil as you take them out of the jar, which leaves them glistening and even more flavorful than they would be without that unctuous touch. But the oil will congeal at refrigerator or cold storage temperatures, so be sure to let the jar and its ingredients come to room temperature to re-liquefy the oil before serving.

INGREDIENTS

1 small head cauliflower (approximately 1 pound)

3 stalks celery

1 red or yellow bell pepper

6 carrots (approximately)

1 medium yellow or white onion

1¾ cups white wine or white distilled vinegar (the wine vinegar has better flavor, but either will show off the colors of the vegetables)

1½ cups water

2 teaspoons kosher or medium-grain sea salt

1 tablespoon sugar or 2 teaspoons honey

2 whole cloves garlic, peeled

1 small, hot chile pepper, pricked with the tip of a knife (optional)

½ teaspoon whole mustard seeds

5 or 6 whole black peppercorns

1 bay leaf

1 sprig fresh thyme (optional)

3–4 tablespoons good-quality extra-virgin olive oil

1. Wash the cauliflower, celery, and bell pepper. Cut out the stem and solid core of the cauliflower and break the rest up into florets that are about an inch thick (a little more is fine). Remove the stem as well as the seeds and any white pith from the pepper. Slice the celery into 1-inch pieces. Slice the bell pepper either into 1-inch pieces or into strips.

2. Wash and peel the carrots, then chop them into 1-inch chunks.

3. Peel the onion. Cut it in half and then into ¼-inch thick slices.

4. Put the vinegar, water, salt, and sugar or honey into a large pot. Bring it to a boil over high heat, stirring to dissolve the salt and sugar or honey.

5. Add the chopped vegetables to the brine. When the liquid returns to a boil, reduce the heat to medium and simmer the vegetables, stirring occasionally, for 5 minutes. Remove the pot from the heat.

6. Put the garlic, hot chile pepper (if using), mustard seeds, and whole black peppercorns into a clean glass quart jar. Use a slotted spoon to transfer the vegetables to the jar. Tuck in the bay leaf and the sprig of thyme (if using) as you add the vegetables—they look nice if they are pressing up against the sides of the jar.

7. Pour the hot brine into the jar. The vegetables and spices should be completely covered by the liquid, but there should still be ¾ inch head space between the surface of the food and the rim of the jar.

8. Pour the extra-virgin olive oil on top of the other ingredients. Add just enough oil to completely coat the surface of the brine. Secure the jar's lid, and put the jar into the refrigerator or cold storage. Wait at least a week for the flavors to develop before sampling.

NOTE

Giardinieri will keep, refrigerated or in cold storage, for at least 3 months. If you want to can it for longer storage (up to a year) at room temperature, leave off the olive oil and process it in a boiling water bath for 15 minutes (adjust the canning time if you live at a high altitude; see the sidebar in the Boiling Water Bath Canning chapter). But the olive oil is such a lovely part of this pickle that I think it's better to include it and make smaller batches that you will eat within 3 months.

Other vegetables that are wonderful when pickled as giardinieri include zucchini, green or wax beans, and romanesco broccoli.

Root Cellaring

Once upon a time, before refrigerators and canning technology were invented, people relied on root cellars to store end-of-the-season crops. Root cellaring is still an effective and energy-efficient way to store hearty fruits and vegetables.

A root cellar is a space—typically underground but at the very least protected from the elements—that maintains a temperature between 35 and 50°F. In other words, well above freezing, but never warm: refrigerator temperatures.

Although commonly called root cellars, these cool temperature storage areas are not only useful for root vegetables. They are also good for storing hearty produce such as cabbage and cauliflower, as well as some types of tree fruit (especially apples and pears, but also quinces, citrus, and others).

TYPES OF ROOT CELLARS

There are hundreds of different designs for root cellars, ranging from the simple "clamp" and basement styles I'm going to describe here, to buried broken refrigerators, to specially designed rooms with hygrometers installed to measure humidity and adjustable vents plus fans on timers (see Useful Resources for root cellar designs from simple to state of the art). What they all have in common is that they take care of the four essentials of cold storage: temperature, humidity, ventilation, and darkness.

Traditional root cellar designs were sometimes extremely simple: just deep holes dug in the ground with a pipe or tunnel for ventilation and earth or or straw piled on top of the food in the hole. A dirt floor was (and still is) the preferred bottom surface of the cellar, although modern root cellars are often floored with concrete.

By the way, most modern basements are far too warm to be used as root cellars unless you wall off a corner and add vents near the bottom and the top that lead directly to outside air.

TIPS FOR SUCCESSFUL ROOT CELLARING

Root cellaring is not quite as simple as having a cool, dark place with good humidity and air circulation in which you store a bunch of fruits and veggies. It isn't complicated, but you will need to include the following practices in your root cellar maintenance.

Harvest vegetables, especially root vegetables, as late in the season as possible before cellaring them. Be very careful when handling food that you intend to cellar. Even minor scratches and bruises can lead to speedy spoilage.

Do not wash root vegetables before putting them into cold storage; simply brush the dirt off of them.

Some foods—potatoes, winter squash including pumpkins, onions, shallots, and garlic—need a drying-out or "curing" period before they are stored in a root cellar. To do this, store them away from direct light at warmish room temperatures for a few days or as much as 2 weeks before transferring them to cold storage.

Carefully examine each fruit or vegetable before putting it into cold storage. Those with bruises, skin breaks, or other blemishes could cause other produce that they are stored with to rot. Ever hear the

BEST FRUITS AND VEGETABLES FOR CELLARING

Apple	Endive	Leek	Potato
Beets	Grapefruit	Lemon	Quince
Cabbage	Horseradish	Orange	Radish
Carrots	Jerusalem artichoke	Parsnip	Rutabaga
Cauliflower	(sunchoke)	Pear	Sweet potato
Celery root (celeriac)	Kohlrabi	Persimmon	Turnip

old adage about one rotten apple spoiling the whole barrel? It's true! Take a look at your cellared fruits and vegetables regularly and remove individual items that are showing any brown spots, mold, or other signs of spoilage. Don't throw them out, though. There's probably plenty of unspoiled food there to salvage for immediate eating, dehydrating, chutney making, and the like.

Vegetables generate heat, which can cause spoilage when they are piled deeply. Try to store the food in single or few layers, and rotate them every couple of weeks.

Apples, pears, and other fruits should be stored separately from vegetables. They should also be loosely, individually wrapped in paper. The reason for both of these pieces of advice is to prevent the ethylene gas emitted by the fruits from speedily ripening adjacent foods or causing them to rot.

Store brassicas including turnips and cabbage separately from other foods—and don't store them too close to your home. This is not because of spoilage factors but rather because this group of vegetables has sulfur compounds that can create an unpleasant rotten egg smell (they'll still taste fine when cooked, but you didn't really want your living room to smell like the Wicked Witch of the West, did you?).

Note: Your root cellar is *not* a good place to store your canned goods. Home-canned jars need a cool but *dry* environment. The relatively high humidity of a root cellar can potentially unseal canning lids.

However, the cool, dry environment that home-canned goods need is an ideal environment for storing onions, shallots, and garlic. Unlike most fruits and vegetables, those members of the *Allium* genus should not be stored in the high humidity of a root cellar. A cool, dark, dry pantry is ideal for storing both your sealed jars of food and those bulb vegetables. If you don't have such a place in your home, prioritize the dark and dry over cool (a hallway closet will work). If you need to store onions, shallots, or garlic in your root cellar, remember that the driest air will be farthest away from the door or opening and at the higher levels.

Two Very Simple Root Cellars

THE CONTAINER CELLAR

This is a basic but highly effective way to build a root cellar using nothing more than a piece of pipe and a garbage can, or any other large, waterproof container (old stand-alone freezers and wooden barrels work great). It is great for preserving both root vegetables and storage variety apples, but remember not to store them together (the apples could cause the veggies to spoil).

Start by digging a hole 2 to 4 inches wider than the width of your container and 6 inches deeper than the container's depth. Set the container into the hole, lid end up. Drill a hole in the lid large enough to hold a ½- to ¾-inch diameter pipe.

Fill the space between the container and the sides of the hole with dirt, using a long stick or shovel handle to pack the dirt down firmly.

Put a thick layer of straw at the bottom of the

container, then start layering in your vegetables or apples, alternating each layer of food with a layer of straw. Try to spread the food out so that none of the pieces are touching.

When the container is two-thirds full, add a pipe to the center sticking straight up and continue layering in food and straw, working around the pipe. Finish with a layer of straw. The pipe needs to be long enough to reach a third of the way down into the layers of food and straw and to stick out above the covered root cellar by 3 inches.

Put on the lid with the pipe sticking up through it. Cut two or more pieces of 2-inch-thick extruded polystyrene foam big enough to cover the lid plus an inch or two beyond the its perimeter. Do not cover the pipe.

Cut a piece of ¾-inch-thick plywood to approximately the same size as the expanse of the foam pieces. Cut out hole for the pipe in the center of the plywood. Fit the plywood over the pipe and weight it down with a few stones.

THE "CLAMP"

This may very well be the original cold storage design. It's definitely one that's been used for many centuries. It's really just an insulated pile of root vegetables with some consideration given to ventilation. A clamp is basic, but it gets the job done in all but the coldest-winter areas.

Any root vegetable that is a candidate for cold storage may be "clamped." Removing damaged vegetables is always important for cold storage, but especially so for this method in which the vegetables will be heaped one on top of the other. Also remove any especially small vegetables, which are likely to wither in a clamp.

Lay out an 8-inch-deep layer of straw directly on outdoor soil in an oblong area several feet long. Pile your sorted produce on top of the straw steeply, ending up with a heap around 35 inches high, give or take. As you lay out the base of the pile of root vegetables, work in horizontal straw tunnels that penetrate the heap and extend slightly beyond it. There should be at least one straw tunnel for every 2 feet (horizontally) of clamp. These tunnels should be at the bottom of the root vegetable heap. Additionally, create vertical straw chimneys at 2-foot intervals along the top of the vegetable heap. The straw tunnels and chimneys will vent gases and excess moisture from the pile of stored food.

Cover the entire mound with another 6 to 8 inches of straw, then cover that with 6 to 8 inches of soil. Take care to leave the ends of the straw tunnels and chimneys uncovered so that air can circulate through them. Pack the soil layer down firmly with your hands or the back of a shovel. Measure the 6 to 8 inches after you've compacted the soil.

Place flat rocks or heavy boards over the straw chimneys. Air will still be able to escape them, but rain won't be able to get in.

When it's time to retrieve some of the food stored in your clamp, choose one spot near the ground on the side of the mound. Use a hand tool such as a trowel to burrow through the outer soil and straw layers. Reach in and take out what you need from the vegetable pile. Fill in the hole you've made with additional straw, and cover that, as before, with 6 to 8 inches of compacted soil.

CHAPTER TEN

Dairy Cultures— Yogurt and Simple Cheeses

Sure, cultured dairy products such as yogurt and cheese add scrumptious flavors and textures, as well as protein, calcium, and other nutrients to our food. But historically, they were also ways to extend the shelf life of milk. If your nanny goat is producing copious quantities of milk, you don't want to waste a drop of it. Make cheese and it will last longer.

Another advantage of making your own dairy products is that you are in control of whether or not to add salt, and whether to go for a whole-milk or low-fat product. You can choose milk from animals that are pastured and healthy, not from industrial "farms" where they are shot full of hormones and antibiotics.

For cheese making, avoid UHT milk. Pastuerized milk will work in these recipes, but UHT-treated milk can fail to form usable curds.

How to Make Yogurt

Arguably, I should've put yogurt in the Fermentation chapter rather than this one. Milk can only become yogurt thanks to the same healthy-for-you, probiotic *Lactobacillus* bacteria that are responsible for vegetable ferments. But I figured most people would look for it in Dairy, so here it is.

Yogurt

COOKING TIME: 20 minutes   WAITING TIME: 8 hours
YIELD: 1 pint; recipe can be doubled

Making your own yogurt is easy. It can also be healthier than store-brand yogurts: Not only can you choose to make it with organic milk from pastured animals, but it won't have any of the thickeners and additives often present in commercially sold yogurts. And even if you flavor your breakfast yogurt with a spoonful of your homemade jam, it will still have less sugar than most store brands of fruit-flavored yogurt.

You also get to skip all those plastic containers.

The first time you make this recipe, you will need to buy some yogurt with active cultures (all commercial brands say on the label if they contain live cultures) to use as your starter culture. Or get some from a yogurt-making friend. Once you've made some, you can use your own homemade yogurt as the starter culture—just always remember to set aside a spoonful of it for this purpose.

INGREDIENTS

1 pint milk (whole, 2 percent, or low-fat*)

1 tablespoon plain yogurt with active yogurt cultures

*I don't recommend using nonfat milk for homemade yogurt because it doesn't set up reliably. Commercial brands add thickeners such as gelatin to give nonfat yogurts a custard-like consistency.

GEAR

Cheese, candy, or meat thermometer

Finely meshed strainer

INSTRUCTIONS

1. Set aside 1 tablespoon yogurt and leave it out to come to room temperature. This is your starter culture. Remember that once you've made this recipe, you can use your own yogurt to start future batches.

2. Pour the milk into a medium-sized pot and gradually heat it over medium-low heat until it reaches 180°F. Turn off the heat and wait for the milk to cool down to between 110 and 106°F.

NOTE

The *Lactobacillus* bacteria that transform milk into yogurt sometimes need a couple of tries to adapt to different types of milk. What this means is that if I switch milk brands, or go from whole milk to 2 percent, the first batch of yogurt I make with the new kind of milk may not be as thick and creamy as subsequent batches will be.

3. While the milk is cooling, wash a glass pint or two half-pint jars and leave them filled with hot water. Do the same with a bowl or pint liquid measuring cup. You want all of the containers the yogurt comes into contact with to be warm.

4. Once the milk cools to 110 to 106°F, empty the hot water out of the bowl or measuring cup. Add the milk and the room-temperature yogurt and whisk to combine. Empty the water out of the jar(s) and pour in the yogurt. Secure the lids.

5. The yogurt needs to spend the next 8 hours at a warm but not hot temperature of approximately 110°F. An old-fashioned oven that has the pilot light perpetually on is perfect. So is an unheated oven with the oven light left on. You can also use a dehydrator set to 110°F with some of the trays removed to make room for the jars. Another possibility is a thermos: Be sure to rinse it out with hot water to warm it before adding the yogurt. And of course, there are special yogurt makers that will maintain this temperature (but don't go out and buy one: They aren't worth the cost).

   It's important not to jostle the jars once they are set in their warm place—that can make the yogurt fail to set up.

6. Put the jar(s) of yogurt in the refrigerator and use within 2 weeks.

Turn Plain Yogurt into Greek Yogurt

If you enjoy the extra-thick, creamy texture of the Greek yogurt that you can buy, you'll be happy to know that it is easy to make your own. Greek yogurt is nothing more than yogurt that has been thickened by straining out some of the whey.

To make it, line a colander or sieve with butter muslin, several layers of cheesecloth, a jelly bag, or even a paper coffee filter. Put the lined colander into a large bowl, or into a sink. Spoon in plain yogurt and let it drain for anywhere from 30 minutes to several hours, depending on how thick you like it.

How to Make Yogurt Cheese (Labneh)

Labneh has a consistency like cream cheese and a similar but slightly tangier taste. It is popular throughout the Middle East, where it is sometimes shaped into balls that are then stored covered with herbs and extra-virgin olive oil.

To make labneh, strain plain yogurt as for Greek yogurt, above, but let it drain for a full 24 to 36 hours in the refrigerator. Transfer the labneh to a covered food storage container. It will keep, refrigerated, for at least a week. For longer storage, cover the surface of the labneh with olive oil before storing it, refrigerated, for up to 1 month.

Ricotta Cheese

PREP TIME: 3 minutes   COOKING TIME: 30 minutes   RESTING TIME: 10 minutes
DRAINING TIME: 30 minutes   YIELD: About 2 cups

Ricotta was originally a sort of something-for-nothing recipe that extracted the last remnants of milk solids from the whey left over from making other kinds of cheese. You can still do that, but you'll only get a scant few spoonfuls of ricotta for your efforts. The procedure detailed here is a bit more extravagant since you start out with whole milk.

This recipe yields plenty of creamy, delicious ricotta that will keep for at least 2 weeks in your refrigerator.

INGREDIENTS

½ gallon whole milk

¾ citric acid dissolved in 2 tablespoons cold water

½ teaspoon salt (optional)

GEAR

Medium pot made of stainless steel or other nonreactive material (no aluminum, copper, or non-enameled cast iron)

Cheese, candy, or meat thermometer

Butter muslin or cheesecloth

INSTRUCTIONS

1. Put the milk and the citric acid water into a medium-sized pot over low heat. Stir in the salt, if using.

2. Whisk or stir the milk mixture frequently to prevent it from scorching on the bottom of the pot. Test the temperature with a meat, cheese, or candy thermometer. When the ingredients have slowly warmed to somewhere between 165 and 190°F, the mixture will separate into curds and whey.

3. Once the curds have formed, remove the ricotta from the heat and let it sit at room temperature for 10 minutes.

4. Line a colander with butter muslin or several layers of cheesecloth and place it in a large bowl. Pour the ricotta into the colander and tie up the ends of the cloth to form a bundle. Hang the bundle of curds somewhere it can drain for 20 to 30 minutes (I tie mine to the kitchen faucet). Go with 20 minutes if you want a softer ricotta, 30 for a firmer version.

5. After the 30 minutes, untie the cloth bundle and transfer the ricotta to a food storage container. It will keep, refrigerated, for up to 2 weeks.

Queso Blanco/ Paneer Cheese

COOKING TIME: 1 hour   DRAINING TIME: 4 hours   YIELD: Approximately 1 pound

---

Queso blanco **is a mild fresh cheese that, like its Indian cousin** *paneer,* **holds its shape when fried, softening slightly but never totally melting.** This makes it ideal for adding to dishes such as Mexican-style beans and greens, or Indian-style *saag paneer*. The reason? Both are curdled with an acidic liquid (vinegar or lemon juice).

Queso fresco, on the other hand, is made with rennet rather than an acid, and does completely melt when heated. Used uncooked and crumbled onto salads, *queso blanco* and *queso fresco* are very similar, but cooked, they are entirely different ingredients.

INGREDIENTS

1 gallon whole milk

¼–⅓ cup white vinegar or lemon juice

GEAR

Large pot made of stainless steel or other nonreactive material (no aluminum, copper, or non-enameled cast iron)

Cheese, candy, or meat thermometer

Butter muslin or cheesecloth

INSTRUCTIONS

1. Pour the milk into a large pot over medium-low heat. Let the milk slowly heat, stirring and checking its temperature often. When it reaches 195°F, slowly stir in the vinegar or lemon juice a little at a time. The curds will begin to separate from the whey (the milk will start to have little lumps of dairy solids, though the whey may still look creamy at this stage). Keep adding small amounts of vinegar or lemon juice until this separation happens.

2. Let the mixture sit in the pot at room temperature for 10 minutes. During this time, the curds and whey will separate more.

3. Line a colander with butter muslin or several layers of cheesecloth. Pour the curds and whey into the colander. Let the curds drain for 1 hour. Tie up the ends of the muslin or cheesecloth, making a tight bundle. Leave the cheese to drain for 3 hours more.

4. Unwrap the cloth and transfer your *queso blanco/ paneer* to a clean container. Store, covered, in the refrigerator or freezer. It keeps for 1 week in the refrigerator, 3 months in the freezer.

Feta Cheese

PREP TIME: 15 minutes   COOKING TIME: 3 hours   BRINING AND DRYING TIME: 38 hours
YIELD: 1–1½ pounds

I am half Greek, and I remember visiting my papou (grandfather) in Corinth as a child. On the floor of a cool alcove just outside the kitchen there was a container a couple of feet tall. In it there was a huge block of feta cheese immersed in water or brine. Eager to get outside and play with my best friend, I used to simply grab a hunk of bread and a big chunk of that feta on the way out the door and call it lunch.

Feta is a great cheese for new cheese makers to try when they're ready for something more advanced than yogurt or ricotta, but still don't want to wait months for the results (as you have to do with many other cheeses).

This homemade feta cheese has a taste and texture that bring me back to my childhood days in Greece. It is especially wonderful when made with goat's milk, if you can get it, but is also good with cow's milk.

INGREDIENTS

1 gallon whole milk (preferably goat's milk)

1 packet mesophilic starter culture*

1½ teaspoons calcium chloride, divided*

½ rennet tablet dissolved in ¼ cup water or ½ teaspoon liquid rennet*

1 pound kosher or other non-iodized salt

2¾ teaspoons white or cider vinegar, divided

*You can get mesophilic starter culture, calcium chloride, and rennet from home cheese-making suppliers—see Useful Resources.

GEAR

Large stainless-steel or other nonreactive pot (no aluminum, copper, or non-enameled cast iron)

Cheese, candy, or digital meat thermometer

Cheese knife or other long-bladed knife such as a bread knife

Cheesecloth or butter muslin

Colander

INSTRUCTIONS

1. Pour the milk into a large pot. Place the pot in a sink and fill the sink with hot water three-quarters of the way up the sides of the pot. Alternatively, you can put the pot full of milk into an even larger pot of hot water. What you're after is a double-boiler effect of very gradually heating the milk—you don't want to put the pot of milk over direct heat. Heat the milk slowly to 86°F.

2. Gently stir in the mesophilic starter culture. Keep the mixture at 86°F for 1 hour. I find it easiest to take the pot out of the surrounding hot water during this hour. It maintains its heat fairly well, but tends to overheat if left in the hot water.

3. Stir in ¼ teaspoon of the calcium chloride.

4. If you're using the rennet tablet, crush it and then dissolve it in ¼ cup of cool water. Add to the milk. If you're using liquid rennet, add it directly to the milk. Gently stir for 1 minute.

5. Leave the mixture alone for 30 minutes, maintaining the 86°F temperature as closely as possible. This may mean putting it back into the sink of hot water for a couple of minutes if it starts to cool off too much.

6. The milk mixture will set up and look something like yogurt. Poke a clean finger about an inch deep into the curd (the semi-solid milk mixture) and gently pull your finger toward you. The curd is set

when it forms a "clean break," separating around your finger rather than staying glommed onto it. It will feel like firm yogurt. If the curd hasn't reached the clean-break stage yet, wait another 30 minutes.

7. Cut the curd with a long-bladed knife. First cut from one side to the other, making slices that go all the way through the curd and are about an inch apart. Turn the pot a quarter turn around and repeat (the second round of slices will cross the first like a tic-tac-toe pattern).

8. Cut the curd one last time by coming in with the knife diagonally across the squares made by your previous slices, at a 45-degree angle to the surface of the curd. This doesn't have to be exact. You want to end up with approximately 1-inch chunks of curd.

9. Stir the chunks of curd very gently. Put the pot back into the sink or larger pot of hot water and gradually raise the temperature to 95°F (you want it to take about an hour). The curds will start to separate from the whey, which is the yellowish liquid you'll see.

10. Line a colander with butter muslin or several layers of cheesecloth. Pour the curds and whey into the colander. Let them drain for 4 hours at room temperature.

11. The curds will congeal together while they drain. Cut the mass that has formed into rough blocks about 3 inches wide and let them drain for another 30 minutes.

12. Make a saturated brine by dissolving approximately 1 pound of kosher or other non-iodized salt in ½ gallon of water. Add the salt ¼ cup at a time, stirring to completely dissolve the salt in between additions. Stop adding salt when it won't dissolve in the water anymore.

13. Stir 1 teaspoon of calcium chloride and 2½ teaspoons of vinegar into the brine.

14. Immerse the blocks of feta in the saturated brine for 10 to 12 hours. Do not leave them in the brine longer than that or you will end up with a feta that is way too salty.

15. Drain the cheese in a colander. Leave it uncovered at room temperature for 2 days, then transfer it to a covered container in the refrigerator. It will keep in the refrigerator for up to 2 weeks. For long-term storage, make a moderately strong brine of 2 tablespoons non-iodized salt dissolved in a pint of water with ¼ teaspoon vinegar and ¼ teaspoon calcium chloride mixed in. Your homemade feta cheese will keep in this brine for several months.

CHAPTER ELEVEN

Preserving in Oil, Butter, and Other Fats

Preserving food in oil or other fats is an ancient method of food preservation. The fat keeps out air, with the result that spoilage is slowed and harmful bacteria and molds are unable to touch the food. This is the method used to preserve duck confit and other potted meats, as well as marinated mushrooms many other foods. It is also why Native American pemmican, an energy-rich trail food made of dried fruit and meat plus fat, keeps so well on long hikes and camping trips.

But as you might recall from the Pressure Canning chapter, botulism spores can survive just fine in moist, anaerobic (oxygen-free) environments. So you need to combine food preservation methods by doing something to the food before you cover it in fat to keep air out. For example, commercial products such as minced garlic in oil are first acidified, and it is the acidity that makes them safe, not the oil. You can achieve the same safe result with non-acidic vegetables and fungi by first briefly exposing them to a vinegar-based brine as I've done with this next recipe. The acidity of the vinegar kills off any harmful bacteria already present on the food, and then the oil prevents air (and new airborne bacteria, yeasts, or molds) from reaching the food. And of course, the combination of the vinegar pretreatment and following up with a good-quality oil not only preserves the food but also adds layers of flavor.

Antipasto Marinated Mushrooms

PREP TIME: 10 minutes   COOKING TIME: 5 minutes   MARINATING TIME: 1 week
YIELD: Approximately 1 quart; recipe can be multiplied

This is how to make those herby, glistening, marinated mushrooms served alongside the *giardinieri* pickled vegetables (recipe in the Cold Storage chapter), olives, and salumi at the start of Italian dinners. It is an easy preservation method that can also be used with many vegetables, including eggplant, zucchini, and cauliflower.

There are three food preservation methods working together to preserve these colorful and delicious hors d'oeuvres. First they get simmered in vinegar, which eliminates any harmful bacteria and also starts to soften and flavor the veggies. Next they get covered in oil, which prevents air from getting to the food, and also adds flavor. Last but not least, they are stored in the refrigerator or another cool place, where the low temperatures delay the oil turning rancid.

INGREDIENTS

1 pound fresh mushrooms

2 cloves garlic

2 small chile peppers (optional)

¼ cup dried tomatoes

3 cups white wine or cider vinegar

1 cup water

1 tablespoon kosher or sea salt

1 teaspoon sugar

Several sprigs fresh herbs (oregano, thyme, savory, and/
or rosemary)

2 bay leaves, fresh or dried

1–1½ cups extra-virgin olive oil

½ teaspoon freshly ground black pepper

INSTRUCTIONS

1. Sterilize two pint jars (sterilizing instructions are in the Boiling Water Bath Canning chapter). They do not necessarily need to be canning jars for this recipe, but they do need to be heatproof.

2. Forget everything you may have heard about never washing mushrooms and just giving them a light brushing: Wash the mushrooms. They won't absorb a lot of water, I promise.

3. Peel and lightly smash the garlic cloves. Pierce the chile peppers (if you're using them) with the tip of a paring knife. Cut the dried tomatoes into ¼-inch-thick strips.

4. Combine the vinegar, water, salt, and sugar in a large pot and bring them to a boil. Add the mushrooms, garlic, chile peppers, and tomatoes. Cook for 4 minutes, stirring often (the mushrooms will float up out of the brine; stirring ensures that all surfaces of the food are exposed to the hot, acidic liquid).

5. Add the herb springs and bay leaves; cook for 1 minute more.

6. Use a slotted spoon to transfer the ingredients to a mixing bowl. Add the extra-virgin olive oil and the black pepper, and stir to coat the food. It's important to use a good-quality oil in this recipe—it's included as much for flavor as it is for food preservation.

7. Use a slotted spoon to divide the still-hot vegetables, herbs, and mushrooms between the two sterilized pint jars. Pour the oil over. The food must be completely immersed in the oil. If it's not, add more extra-virgin olive oil until it is.

8. Tightly cover the jars and let them sit at room temperature until they are no longer warm. Transfer jars of marinated mushrooms to a cool, dark place—your refrigerator, an unheated garage if it's winter, or the like. Note that because of their high humidity, root cellars are not good places to store food preserved in oil.

9. Wait at least 2 weeks for the flavors to develop before digging in. The olive oil will congeal into a solid fat when it is cold, so bring the jars into a warm room and wait for the olive oil to return to a liquid state before serving.

Duck Confit

PREP TIME: 5 minutes   CURING TIME: 24 hours   COOKING TIME: 4 hours

YIELD: 1 pint; recipe can be multiplied

Duck confit is duck slowly cooked in its own fat until it is fall-off-the-bone tender. It is then stored in that cooking fat until you are ready to use it. It is an essential ingredient for the cassoulet of southwestern France, and can also transform a simple salad into a feast.

Although duck is the poster ingredient for confit, it is entirely possible to turn other things into confit. The reason ducks are so often chosen is that they have more fat than other animals (it helps them float when they are paddling in water).

You could made duck confit with no ingredients other than the duck, but it's even better after an initial salting and with the addition of thyme or other herbs.

INGREDIENTS

⅓ cup kosher salt

1 tablespoon sugar

1 teaspoon dried thyme or 1 tablespoon fresh thyme

1 teaspoon freshly ground black pepper

⅛ teaspoon freshly ground nutmeg

1 teaspoon curing salt (optional; see *Useful Resources*)

1 pound duck legs (or any other bone-in, fatty duck parts except the breasts)

2 bay leaves

⅛ cup olive oil or rendered duck or chicken fat

HOW TO MAKE CONFIT

Another technique that combines more than one method of food preservation method is to first cook the food in fat over several hours, then store it covered by the cooking fat. The heat of the cooking kills off any remaining harmful bacteria, and then storing the food in the cooking fat keeps air from reaching the food. Sometimes, as with duck confit, an initial salt cure adds a third preservation method to the mix. As with all of the recipes in this chapter, it is important to store the final product in the refrigerator or freezer to slow or prevent the fat from turning rancid.

INSTRUCTIONS

1. Combine the salt, sugar, thyme, pepper, nutmeg, and curing salt (if using) in a large bowl or container.

2. Rub the salt-and-seasoning mixture into the pieces of duck. Be sure to get it rubbed into every surface and cranny. Cover and refrigerate for 24 hours.

3. Preheat the oven to 225°F.

4. Brush as much of the salt mixture off of the duck as possible. Do not rinse: You want the duck to be dry for the next step.

5. Place the duck pieces, skin-side down in a baking dish. Tuck the bay leaves under them. Spoon in the duck or chicken fat, or pour the olive oil over the duck.

6. Bake the duck for 1 hour. During that time the fat will start to render out of the duck. If the duck pieces are not completely covered by the fat after 1 hour, add additional fat or oil. The duck must be completely immersed in fat for the rest of the confit process or it will not be safely preserved.

7. Bake for an additional 2 to 5 hours. The meat should almost fall off the bone when you try to lift out a piece of duck.

8. You can put the whole pieces of duck confit into a heatproof container and pour the hot liquid fat over, or you can strip the meat off the bones first. Either way, run a table knife or spoon around the sides of the container and press down gently on the top of the duck to release any air bubbles. Make sure the duck is completely covered by the fat. Refrigerated duck confit keeps for 3 months. You can also freeze it for up to 1 year.

"Confit" Vegetables

PREP TIME: 5 minutes   COOKING TIME: 3–4 hours
YIELD: 1½ pints; recipe can be multiplied

I know some food geeks out there will correct me and say that this is not a _real_ confit. But _confit_ has become a verb as well as a noun for most chefs (and an increasing number of home cooks). It is in that way—as a verb—that I use the word here. The method can be used with any fairly sturdy vegetable, including all root vegetables and some hearty buds and stalks such as artichoke hearts, celery, and burdock flower stalks.

The result is an unctuous treat that transforms pasta sauces, and also makes a quick hors d'oeuvre (just put a dab on a cracker or toast point). You could also use it to replace duck confit and make a vegetarian cassoulet.

INGREDIENTS

1 pound vegetables, peeled if necessary

2 teaspoons salt

½ teaspoon sugar (optional)

½ teaspoon dried thyme _or_ 1½ teaspoons fresh thyme leaves

½ teaspoon ground black pepper

Approximately 1 pint extra-virgin olive oil

INSTRUCTIONS

1. Preheat the oven to 225°F.

2. Peel root vegetables if necessary. Cut the vegetables into ½- to 1-inch pieces.

3. Put the vegetables into a baking dish and toss with the salt, sugar, thyme, and black pepper. Cover the vegetables completely in extra-virgin olive oil.

4. Bake the vegetables, uncovered, for 3 to 4 hours. There should be some bubbles forming and rising to the surface as the water in the vegetables evaporates, but it should never reach a boil.

5. Spoon the still-hot vegetable confit into sterilized, heatproof jars. Press down on the food gently with the back of a spoon to release any air bubbles. The vegetables must be completely immersed in the oil.

6. Vegetable confit will last in the refrigerator, tightly covered, for at least 3 months. Unlike duck and meat confits, it does not freeze well.

Herb Butter

PREP TIME: 5 minutes   YIELD: ½ cup

Herb butters can look elegant and taste luxurious, but they are actually so easy to make and use that they deserve to become part of your everyday meals. Use herb butter with steamed vegetables, baked potatoes, fish, and anything else that a savory butter flavor might enhance.

INGREDIENTS

½ cup unsalted butter

1–3 sprigs fresh herbs (chervil, chives, parsley, sage, rosemary, and thyme—song reference intended—are all excellent candidates for herb butter)

½ teaspoon grated lemon zest (optional)

½–1 teaspoon salt

INSTRUCTIONS

1. Leave the butter out at room temperature for 30 minutes to soften.

2. Mince the fresh herbs and grate the lemon zest (if you're using it).

3. Use a fork to mash together the butter, minced herbs, and zest. Mash in salt to taste.

4. Put the herb butter onto a piece of parchment or waxed paper. Roll it up in the paper so that it forms a little log. Put the paper-wrapped herb butter log into the additional wrapping of a plastic bag or

other food storage container.

    Herb butter will keep in the refrigerator for up to 2 months, or in the freezer for up to 6 months. The butter will still be edible after that, but the quality will decline. When you're using frozen herb butters, transfer them to the refrigerator 24 hours before you plan on using them.

Rosemary Oil

PREP TIME: 2 minutes   INFUSING TIME: 1 hour   YIELD: 1 cup

This is my go-to pantry item for roasting root vegetables and winter squash, pan-frying potatoes, and even drizzling on popcorn instead of butter. I cannot imagine my kitchen without it.

Making rosemary oil is different from most other recipes that aim to capture the flavor of the volatile aromatic essential oils in herbs. The usual advice is to minimize the amount of time the herbs are exposed to heat and air so that those essential oils don't evaporate. But rosemary's resinous aroma and taste holds up better to heat than most leafy herbs, which is why this method works.

Unlike basil oil (see the Freezing chapter), which is a puree of fresh leaves in oil, this is an infused oil. The rosemary leaves get strained out once they have imparted their flavor.

The key to making this simple recipe fabulous is the quality of the extra-virgin olive oil you use. While it's not necessary to use an ultra-expensive oil, it's also important not to skimp too much here. The oil is as much a part of the flavor as the rosemary.

INGREDIENTS

1 cup good quality extra-virgin olive oil

¼ cup fresh rosemary leaves

INSTRUCTIONS

1. Strip the rosemary leaves off the twigs by holding the growing tip end in one hand and pulling down the length of the twig toward the base with the other.

2. Put the rosemary leaves into either a slow cooker or a small saucepan. Add the oil.

3. If you're using a slow cooker, put it on the high setting and let the rosemary cook in the oil, uncovered, for 1 hour. If you're using a saucepan, put it on the stove over low heat until the oil is warm and you start to see a few bubbles rising to the surface. Do not let the oil smoke or come to a full simmer. Turn off the heat and let the rosemary steep in the oil for 1 hour.

4. Strain out the rosemary. If you made the oil in a slow cooker, let it cool for 20 minutes. Funnel the rosemary oil into clean glass bottles and cover tightly. It will keep at room temperature for at least 2 months. For longer storage, keep it in the refrigerator (the olive oil will congeal in the refrigerator's cold temperatures, so take the oil out at least half an hour before you want to use it so that it can re-liquefy).

Pemmican

Pemmican is a concentrated, high-energy, and high-protein snack food that will keep for many months if stored in a cool place. *Pemmican* is a Cree word that means "rendered fat." The fat you use can be saved bacon drippings, rendered chicken fat, purchased or homemade beef suet, or any other animal fat.

INGREDIENTS

2 pounds lean ground meat (beef, turkey, venison, etc.)

1–2 cups rendered fat (suet, bacon fat, etc.)

3 cups finely chopped dried fruit

¼ cup honey (optional)

¼ cup finely chopped nuts (optional)

INSTRUCTIONS

1. Spread out the ground meat on parchment paper either on the racks of a dehydrator or on a baking sheet. Dry at 180°F overnight or for about 8 hours. You want the meat to be crispy-dry for pemmican, not chewy as for jerky.

2. Pulverize the meat until it is almost a powder. You can use a mortar and pestle, but feel free to take advantage of a blender or food processor to do the job.

3. Melt the fat over medium-low heat in a small pot.

4. Combine the meat powder, chopped dried fruit, and the honey and nuts (if using). Add the liquefied fat a little bit at a time, working in each addition with your clean hands. Keep adding fat until the pemmican holds together when you squeeze a small handful of it. Use only as much fat as necessary to hold the mixture together.

5. Put the pemmican onto a dish or tray and pat it out until it's in a layer about ½ inch thick. Chill it in the refrigerator or another cool place until it is solid enough to cut into bars that are about 4 inches long and 1 or 2 inches wide.

6. Wrap the pemmican pieces individually in waxed or parchment paper and store in the refrigerator or another cool place.

CHAPTER TWELVE

Preserving in Alcohol

Like lacto-fermentation, alcoholic fermentation is a process in which live organisms act on existing substances in the starter food or juice and transform them. To hugely simplify a process that many artisans devote their lives to fine-tuning, alcohol is the result of live yeasts working on sugars. The yeast activity transforms glucose into pyruvic acid and finally into ethanol.

The reason grapes have become synonymous with wine, even though wine can be made from other fruits, is that grapes naturally possess the right combination of sugar, acidity, and natural yeast to produce a balanced fermented product. That's why the archaic stomp-and-wait method of winemaking worked. Fruits other than grapes may require additions of sugar, yeast, or acid in order to successfully ferment.

Distilled alcohol starts out with a naturally fermented product such as wine. Using equipment that can expose the fermented liquid to heat and evaporation without losing any of the alcohol, distillation raises the percentage of alcohol in the final product.

Distilled alcohol is extremely antimicrobial, and extremely stable, and that is why it can be used to preserve food long-term. Lower-alcohol products such as wine or beer, when exposed to air, tend to be visited by the acetic acid bacteria that convert alcohol into vinegar (there is no such thing as vinegar that was not first an alcoholic brew). But distilled alcoholic beverages including the brandy, rum, and vodka used in some of the recipes below are extremely stable.

Brandied Peaches

PREP TIME: 20 minutes   CANNING TIME: 20 minutes   YIELD: 2 pints

---

These peaches are wonderful on top of desserts (try brandied peaches on top of a hot peach or apple pie—yum!), but they are also great companions for pork, duck, or game meats (similar to serving applesauce with a pork chop, only better). And after all the fruit is eaten, enjoy sipping the peach-infused brandy as a warming taste of summer during the cold months.

This recipe also works well with plums and other tree fruits. You can leave out the spices or vary them, increase or decrease the amount of sugar to taste. The alcohol is the main thing that is safely preserving the fruit. I've given canning instructions here, but you could simply refrigerate them instead if you've got the refrigerator space. They will also keep just fine in a cold cellar.

INGREDIENTS

3 pounds ripe peaches

2 cups 80-proof brandy

1½ cups sugar or 1 cup light honey (clover, orange blossom, or wildflower is good here)

2 cinnamon sticks (optional)

2 whole cloves (optional)

Two 1-inch pieces of vanilla bean pod (optional)

1. Bring a large pot of water to a boil. Prepare a large bowl of ice water.

2. Cut a small X in the bottom of each peach with a paring knife. When the water is at a full rolling boil, carefully put the peaches into the water. Let the fruits blanch for 1 minute before lifting them out with a slotted spoon and transferring them to the bowl of ice water. Let them sit in the ice water for 5 minutes.

3. While the peaches are chilling, heat the brandy and the sugar or honey in a medium-sized pot over low heat, stirring to dissolve. Remove the pot from the heat as soon as the ingredients have liquefied and combined (do not let the mixture come to a boil, or even to a simmer).

4. Peel the peaches and remove the pits. If they are freestone peaches, you should be able to slice around the fruit and then twist it free of the pit in neat halves. If they are clingstone, don't drive yourself crazy trying to get halves. Instead, use a paring knife to slice pieces of the peaches off the pits.

5. Put the peach pieces into clean pint-sized canning jars. Slip in the spices, if using, as you add the fruit. Pack the fruit in fairly tightly, leaving 1 inch of head space. Pour the brandy syrup over the other ingredients, completely covering the fruit and this time leaving just ½ inch of head space.

6. Wipe the rims of the jars clean and dry with a cloth or paper towel. Screw on the canning lids. Process in a boiling water bath for 20 minutes (adjust the canning time if you live at a high altitude; see the sidebar in the Boiling Water Bath Canning chapter).

7. Wait at least a month for the flavors to develop before enjoying your brandied peaches.

Rumtopf

The beauty of a classic *rumtopf* is that you add each kind of fruit as it comes into season. So the jar may start with late spring's strawberries and juneberries, but get topped with summer's plums and blackberries, and then autumn's pears or other fruit.

Rumtopf started in late spring is ready to serve during December's holidays, but tastes significantly better if you let it age until the *following* year's holidays. For that reason, I like to keep two batches of rumtopf going: the one I'm adding to this year, and the one I made last year to serve this year.

Any of the following work well in rumtopf: apricots, blackberries, cherries, grapes, peaches, pears, plums, raspberries, and strawberries. Some rumtopf recipes include pineapple, but I find that it overwhelms the flavors of the other fruits. You can also add raisins or other dried fruit.

INGREDIENTS

Seasonal fruit (see the headnote above)

108-proof rum

1 cup sugar per pound of fruit

INSTRUCTIONS

1. Start with a 1-gallon, widemouth glass canning jar or with a 1- to 3-gallon ceramic crock (you can buy special rumtopf crocks, but it's really not necessary). Sprinkle each pound of fruit you put in with a cup of sugar. Pour in rum to cover the fruit.

2. You'll need to keep the fruit submerged in the rum. You can do this by putting plastic wrap or waxed paper directly on the surface of the liquid, or, if the container is wide enough, by weighting the fruit down. A plate that can fit inside the container with a closed jar full of water on top of the plate works well.

3. Keep adding different fruits, with additional rum and sugar each time, as they come into season.

4. Once the jar is full, cover it and store it away from direct light. Age it for a minimum of 3 months before serving. Before that, the flavor can be harsh, but as it ages it becomes deliciously mellow.

5. After the rumtopf has aged, use a slotted spoon to lift out the boozy fruit and use it to top ice cream, cakes, custards, puddings and other desserts. Once the fruit is gone, serve the fruit-infused rum as a digestif or use it in cocktails.

Limoncello

PREP TIME: 15 minutes   COOKING TIME: 5 minutes   INFUSING TIME: 2–4 weeks
YIELD: 2 750ml bottles

This sunshine-yellow, lightly sweet liqueur has a vibrant citrus flavor. It is usually credited to Sorrento, Italy, but its non-Italian vodka base suggests that either limoncello is a fairly recent invention, or it was traditionally made with some other form of alcohol.

Limoncello is very easy to make, and wonderful as a chilled digestif. It can be mixed with sparkling water for a refreshing summer drink.

INGREDIENTS

10–12 organically grown (pesticide-free) lemons
1 750ml bottle vodka (100 proof if possible, but 80 proof will work)
2½ cups water
1½ cups sugar

INSTRUCTIONS

1. Wash the lemons and then use a vegetable peeler to remove the yellow zest of the peels. You will be using the strips of yellow zest to make the limoncello. The now naked lemons can be stored in a container in the refrigerator, but plan on using their juice in another recipe soon because they won't keep long.

2. Put the strips of yellow lemon zest into a large, clean glass jar.

3. Pour the vodka over the strips of lemon zest (save the bottle for Step 6). The lemon should be completely submerged in the vodka; push it down with a spoon if necessary. Cover the jar and leave it at room temperature for 2 weeks. Shake the jar every other day to redistribute the lemon peels.

4. After the 2 weeks, the liquid will have taken on a bright yellow color from the lemon peel strips. Pour the mixture through a strainer into a large bowl or pitcher. Discard the peels.

5. Combine the water and sugar in a pot over medium heat. Cook, stirring, until the sugar has dissolved into the water to form a simple syrup. As soon as the sugar has dissolved, remove the pot from the heat. Let the syrup cool to room temperature (if you're in a hurry you can put it in the refrigerator to speed the cooling process).

6. Pour the lemon-infused vodka into the syrup and stir to combine. Pour the limoncello through a funnel into two clean 750ml glass bottles (one of them can be the empty vodka bottle left over from step 3). Cap or cork tightly.

7. Store your bottles of limoncello in the refrigerator or freezer. There's still one ingredient left to add: patience. Wait at least 2 weeks, preferably a month for the flavors of your limoncello to mix and mellow before serving.

Raspberry Cordial

PREP TIME: 30 minutes   COOKING TIME: 30 minutes   WAITING TIME: 2 hours

YIELD: Approximately 1 quart

If you start a batch of this cordial when late summer's berry harvest is at its peak, the ruby-colored brew will be ready to sip by the holiday season. But since you can use fresh or frozen fruit for this recipe, you could make it at any time of year. This recipe works equally well with blackberries and wild brambleberry (*Rubus*) species such as wineberry and purple flowering raspberry.

INGREDIENTS

2 quarts fresh or frozen raspberries, blackberries, or other edible *Rubus* spp. fruits

2 cups boiling water

2 cups sugar (stick to granulated sugar if the color of the final product is important to you)

INSTRUCTIONS

1. If you are using frozen berries, thaw them before proceeding with the recipe. Use a potato masher or the bottom of a wine bottle to crush the fruit in a large nonreactive (no aluminum, copper, or un-enameled cast iron) pot or mixing bowl.

2. Pour in the boiling water and stir well. Cover the
    pot or bowl with a dish towel and leave it out at
    room temperature for 24 hours. Stir several times
    during that period.

3. Strain the berry mash through a finely meshed
    sieve or through a colander lined with cheesecloth.
    Save the strained liquid.

4. Add the sugar and stir until it is completely dis-
    solved. Stir again every 15 minutes for 1 hour (five
    times total).

5. Strain the mash again through a colander lined
    with several layers of damp cheesecloth.

6. Funnel the liquid into a clean wine bottle. Do not
    cork or seal the bottles yet: They could explode
    during fermentation. Instead, seal the bottles ei-
    ther with a fermentation lock (see *Gear and Useful
    Resources*), or with a pricked balloon.

If you're using a fermentation lock, the
bubbling action of peak fermentation will subside
within a couple of months. If you're going the balloon route, prick it once with a pin. The pinprick
will allow the gases produced by fermentation to
escape so that the balloon (and the bottle) doesn't
explode. The balloon will still inflate during the
active fermentation period, though. When it eventually deflates, fermentation is complete and you
can proceed to the next step.

If there are no signs of fermentation after the
first 2 days (the raspberry mixture should be very
frothy on top), add a scant pinch of wine or baking
yeast (really scant, like just a few grains).

7. After approximately 2 months, fermentation
    should have ceased or subsided. Cap or cork the
    bottle tightly. Store it on its side in a dark, cool
    place for 2 more months.

8. When you first open the cordial to serve it, it may
    still be slightly fizzy. It is at its best decanted to
    stillness (this just takes an hour or so). I recommend
    decanting the whole bottle and then storing it in
    clear glass vessel that shows off its gorgeous color.

Elderflower Champagne

PREP TIME: 10 minutes   INITIAL FERMENTATION TIME: 48 hours   FULL FERMENTATION TIME: 3 weeks
YIELD: 4 quarts/liters

Okay, technically I can't call this "champagne" because it isn't made from champagne grapes. But like true champagne, it is vigorously fizzy. Elderflower champagne relies for fermentation on natural yeasts present on the flowers, and is ready to drink just a few weeks from making it. You can use fresh or dried elderflowers for this recipe.

You'll need to use plastic water or soda bottles, or thick glass champagne-style bottles for this recipe. Did I mention that the fermentation is vigorous? Regular glass bottles could explode (it's happened to me, and the cleanup is not fun).

INGREDIENTS

1½ pounds sugar or 1 pound honey

2 pints boiling non-chlorinated or filtered water

6 pints cold non-chlorinated or filtered water

¼ cup apple cider vinegar or the juice and rind of 2 large lemons plus 2 tablespoons apple cider vinegar

INSTRUCTIONS

1. The natural yeasts present on the elderberry flowers are responsible for the successful fermentation of this brew, so don't wash the flower heads. Do shake them vigorously to dislodge and remove any insects.

2. Put the sugar or honey into a large bowl or ceramic crock. Pour in the 2 pints of boiling water. Stir until the sugar or honey is completely dissolved.

3. Stir in the 6 pints of cold water, along with the vinegar or lemon-juice-and-vinegar combination. Add the lemon rind, if using. Strip the florets off of the elderberry flower clusters into the liquid mixture. Discard the inedible stalks.

4. Cover the bowl or crock with a clean dish towel. Let the mixture sit at room temperature for 48 hours, and stir it at least twice a day. By the second day, you should see the frothy, bubbly signs of fermentation, especially right after you give the mixture a stir. If there are no signs of fermentation after 48 hours, add a tiny pinch of wine or baking yeast and wait another 48 hours, stirring every few hours, before proceeding with the recipe.

5. Strain the elderflower champagne mash through a finely meshed sieve or a colander lined with several layers of cheesecloth.

6. Funnel the brew into clean plastic soda or water bottles with screw tops, or into thick ceramic bottles with flip tops (some artisinal beers come in this type of bottle). Leave at least an inch of head space between the surface of the liquid and the rims of the bottles. Secure the tops.

7. Leave at room temperature for a week, "burping" (opening briefly) the bottles at least once a day. After the week at room temperature, move them to the refrigerator, but keep burping the bottles occasionally for another week.

Dandelion Wine

PREP TIME: 1 hour   COOKING TIME: 15 minutes   YIELD: 3½ quarts/liters

---

Dandelion wine has a sort of a mythical status in that almost everyone has heard of it, but very few people have ever actually tasted it. It's not difficult to make, but it does require time: time to pick enough flowers for the recipe, patience waiting for the wine to mature. Although the recipe includes sugar, it gets fermented out and the result is a dry wine with a color like sunshine.

INGREDIENTS

2 quarts dandelion flowers

1 gallon filtered or non-chlorinated water

Zest and juice of 3 lemons (but not the seeds or bitter white inner peel)

Zest and juice of 3 oranges (again, not the seeds or bitter white inner peel)

1½ pounds sugar

¾ pound golden raisins, chopped

1 teaspoon yeast nutrient (see Useful Resources) or 2 tablespoons cornmeal

1 packet wine yeast (see Useful Resources) or ½ teaspoon baking yeast

INSTRUCTIONS

1. Use scissors to snip off most of the calyces (green parts) from the base of the dandelion stems. Compost or discard those green parts and the stems. Don't worry if a few specks of green make their way into the recipe along with the yellow flowers, but remember that too much of the green parts will result in a bitter wine. Put the trimmed flowers into a nonreactive crock, pot, or other vessel (no aluminum, copper, or non-enameled iron).

2. In a separate pot, bring the water to a boil. Pour it over the flowers and then let the flowers infuse in the hot water for 2 hours. Strain through a jelly bag or a colander lined with several layers of cheesecloth or one layer of butter muslin. Squeeze to extract as much of the juice as possible. The spent dandelion flowers are great for your compost. Reserve the strained liquid.

3. Bring the dandelion flower infusion to a boil in a large pot over high heat. Stir in the citrus zests and juices, and the sugar. Stir to help the sugar dissolve.

4. Stir in the chopped raisins. Remove the pot from the heat and let the contents cool to room temperature.

5. Stir in the yeast nutrient or cornmeal along with the wine or baking yeast. Cover the mixture and leave it at room temperature for 10 to 14 days. During that time, stir it at least three times a day (you can't stir too often).

6. Sterilize a glass gallon jug by filling it with solution of 1 tablespoon bleach in a gallon of water, or with an oxygen-based sterilizer such as One-Step available from home wine-making suppliers. Drain and rinse the jug. Strain the dandelion concoction through a strainer and a funnel into the jug. Seal the jug with either a fermentation lock or a balloon with a single pinprick in it. Both the fermentation lock and the pricked balloon allow gases to escape while preventing harmful bacteria and mold from getting in.

7. After 1 month, siphon or carefully pour off the liquid into another sanitized jug, leaving behind the yeasty "lees," or sediment at the bottom of the first jug. If there is more than 2 inches of air space between the top of the wine and the rim of the new jug, top it off with a simple syrup made of equal parts water and sugar. Top as before with a fermentation lock or pricked balloon.

8. Repeat this siphoning off again every 3 months, leaving the lees behind each time, until the wine is clear rather than cloudy and there is no longer any yeasty sediment forming on the bottom of the jug.

9. Funnel the wine into sterilized wine bottles. Cork the bottles: I recommend getting a hand corker from a winemaking supply company (see Useful Resources). They are inexpensive and do a much better job of securely corking the bottles than you can do without one. Store the bottles on their sides in a cool, dark place for at least one year before drinking.

Brandied or Fermented Sour Cherries

PREP TIME: 30 minutes   MACERATION TIME: 2 hours   FERMENTATION TIME: 2–4 weeks
YIELD: 1 quart; recipe can be multiplied

I first came across a version of this recipe in an old church club cookbook. The recipe was titled Brandied Cherries, so I assumed the cherries would be preserved by the high alcohol content of brandy. It turns out that brandying is an old-fashioned verb referring to this particular method of fermenting fruit. The result is somewhere between a pickled cherry and a boozy one, and absolutely delicious, especially when served with a soft, stinky cheese such as Camembert.

It is important to use sour cherries for this recipe. I've tried it with sweet cherries, and although the fermentation worked, the final flavor was bland. Look for sour cherries at farmers' markets during the few weeks that they are in season in summer.

This recipe makes a quart, but you can make larger batches in a fermentation crock or other large container. For bigger batches, weigh the sour cherries after they have been stemmed and pitted, and use a ratio of equal parts sour cherries and sugar by weight.

INGREDIENTS

3 pounds sour cherries

2 pounds sugar

GEAR

Cherry pitter

Crock or widemouth quart jar

INSTRUCTIONS

1. Wash the lemons and then use a vegetable peeler Wash the sour cherries and remove the stems. Remove the pits (I strongly recommend using a cherry or olive pitter—it makes this task easier).

2. Weigh the stemmed and pitted sour cherries. Put them into a large bowl and add an equal amount of sugar by weight (more or less than 2 pounds). Stir to combine the fruit and sugar.

3. Cover the crock or bowl with a dish towel. Let the mixture sit for 2 hours, during which the sugar will start to dissolve and to draw the juices out of the cherries.

4. Stir well to dissolve any sugar that hasn't liquefied yet. Put a weight on top of the cherries to keep them submerged in the syrup. Cover the crock or container and leave it at room temperature for 2 to 4 weeks, stirring at least once a day (you can't stir too many times). During this time the cherries will start to ferment vigorously, and foam will froth up when you stir them. Wait until the fermentation has slowed and there isn't as much frothy activity before proceeding to the next step.

5. Use a slotted spoon to transfer the now fermented sour cherries to a clean glass quart jar (or more than one smaller jar). Pour enough of the syrup over the fruit to completely cover it. Secure the lid, and store the cherries in the coldest part of your refrigerator, or in a cold cellar.

CHAPTER THIRTEEN

Troubleshooting

Lacto-Fermentation Foes

FERMENTATION NEVER BEGINS, OR THE FOOD SPOILS EVEN AFTER FERMENTATION SEEMED TO START

If after 1 to 3 days at a room temperature (somewhere between 60 and 85°F), your ferment still hasn't started fermenting, you may have to compost it and start over. Definitely if the food smells bad (it should have a lightly sour smell when fermenting, not a rotten one), or if there are strings of cloudy muck in the liquid, the batch has spoiled and should be discarded. Note that mold is *not* necessarily a reason to abandon your ferment (see below).

Two things that can help prevent both a non-starting ferment and a spoiled one are adjusting the amount of salt according to the ambient temperature, and/or including a live culture starter from whey (such as that from strained yogurt; see the Dairy chapter).

THERE'S SCUM ON TOP OF YOUR FERMENTS

Assuming that all the signs (non-moldy, frothy bubbling and a clean, lightly sour smell) of healthy fermentation have occurred or are occurring, any scum that forms on top of ferments is harmless and can simply skimmed away. You can also simply remove the top layer of the fermented food: What is underneath is usually in perfect condition.

Canning Woes

YOUR JARS DON'T SEAL

There are four main reasons why a canning jar may fail to seal after boiling water bath or pressure canning.

The first is overfilling the jars. If you left less than the amount of head space (the space between the surface of the food and the rim of the jar) specified in the recipe, a good vacuum seal won't form. If the recipe instructions don't specify an amount of head space, then between ½ and ¾ inch is a good all-purpose distance to use. This also happens to be the distance between the rim of the jar and the ridges just below its screwband section, which makes it easy to measure.

The next reason why a jar may not seal is that there was some food or liquid on the rim of the jar. This can prevent the adhesive ring on the underside of the lid from fastening on. To prevent this from happening, always wipe the rims of the jars clean after you have filled them with the food you are canning. Use a moist, clean cloth or paper towel.

The third reason a jar may fail to seal is that the canning lid is defective. This can happen with new lids—it is rare, but it does happen. More likely is that you reused a canning lid. With two-piece lids you can reuse the screw-on ring, but not the central disk. Single-piece lids are not supposed to be reused at all. The reason is that previous use may have worn out the adhesive ring, or there may be some barely noticeable dent or bend that could prevent a seal.

The last reason why a jar may not seal is that there is a tiny chip or crack in its rim. Always carefully examine each jar before using it, and recycle any that have chips or cracks. This is especially true of jars that you have reused many times, or that you purchased secondhand from a garage sale or thrift shop.

WHAT TO DO WITH A JAR THAT DIDN'T SEAL

You took the jars out of the canner, and as they cooled all but one of them sealed. What do you do with that unsealed jar? You have two options. The first is to simply store it in the refrigerator immediately and eat the contents within a week. The second is to reprocess the jar with a new lid. To do this, you'll need to first empty the jar, reheat the contents to a boil, clean the jar, and refill it with the food. Be sure to leave enough head space, wipe the rim of the jar clean, and use a fresh lid before reprocessing in a boiling water bath or pressure canner according to the recipe instructions. Keep in mind that when food is heat-processed more than once, both its nutritional content and quality of texture and taste decline. These two ways of handling an unsealed jar only apply to jars that were freshly canned. It's a whole different story if a jar originally sealed, but when you take it off the shelf weeks or months later, it isn't sealed anymore. The best response in this case is to throw the food out.

A JAR BREAKS IN PROCESSING

You open the canner to find broken glass and food floating in the hot water. Or everything looks fine until you reach in with your jar lifter to lift one out and the entire bottom drops off the jar. Not fun. Here are the three possible explanations of what went wrong, and how to prevent a repeat experience.

The most likely culprit is a hairline crack in the jar that you didn't notice when you got it out for your canning project. As I mentioned in the unsealed jars notes above, always inspect jars to make sure they are free from cracks or chips before using them.

Another possibility is too sudden of a temperature shift. Although canning jars are designed to withstand high heat, if they are cold when you pour in boiling-hot food, or the jar and the food in it are hot but water in the canner is cold, or any other sudden jolt occurs from hot to cold (or vice versa), the jar may crack. Often this will be a hard-to-spot hairline crack that you won't notice until the jar breaks during processing. Always fill empty jars with hot water to heat them, then pour the water out before adding hot food. Make sure the water in the canner is equally hot before adding the jars of hot food.

One last reason why jars could break during boiling water bath or pressure canning is that you didn't put a rack or towel in the bottom of the canner before adding the jars. The glass jars bounce around a bit during processing, so you need to place a buffer between their bottoms and both the metal bottom of the canner and the heat source directly under it. If you

follow the canning instructions on given in this book, this won't be an issue.

FRUIT FLOATS AND DISCOLORS

The peaches floated up out of their canning syrup, or the tomatoes separated from their juices and are now suspended above an unappealing watery layer, or the picked green beans rose out of their brine. None of these jars is attractive. Worse yet, the fruit pieces or vegetables that rose above their canning liquid into the head space below the lid may turn brown. Yuck.

Now, if the food was processed according to instructions and the jars successfully sealed, the food inside is safe to eat. Still, it isn't very enticing when the color has gone off or the solids separated from the liquids (it's true that we eat first with our eyes!). To prevent these problems, the first thing you want to do is keep the fruits or vegetables from floating up out of the canning liquid. Once out of the canning liquid, many ingredients have a tendency to brown.

The first solution works when you are dealing with relatively long pieces of food that you are going to stack vertically in the jars, such as green beans, carrot spears, or cucumbers. Be sure to pack the food in tightly. Really tightly: Keep shoving the pieces in until you can't find room for even one more. This is especially important for recipes such as pickles that start out with raw vegetables in the jars: They will shrink a bit during the canning process.

That leads directly to the second solution for float and discoloration, which is not to raw pack ingredients for canning. For fruit, tomatoes, and vegetables that do not need to be crisp (in other words, those that will be pressure canned in a plain salt brine or chopped and cooked into a soft-textured recipe such as chutney), I recommend hot packing. Hot packing means that you cook the food a little bit before transferring it to the jars. This single step goes a long way toward preventing float and discoloration.

Even so, you may end up with a little bit of separation in the jars between the solid food on top and the liquid on the bottom. Once the jars are *completely* cooled and the lids firmly sealed, you can redistribute the contents of the jars by lightly shaking them. But it is really important that you do this only after the ingredients are entirely cooled and sealed, or you could actually prevent or undo a safe seal.

Pickling Predicaments

"HELP! MY GARLIC TURNED BLUE"

Pickled garlic will sometimes turn blue. This is the result of an enzymatic reaction that occurs occasionally when the sulfur compounds in garlic are exposed to oxygen and then to an acidic environment such as a vinegar-based pickle brine. The bright blue color may seem alarming, but actually it is harmless and the pickles—including the blue garlic—are still perfectly safe to eat.

MUSHY PICKLES

Crunch defines pickles just as much as their tangy taste, so it's no fun when your pickles turn out mushy.

While there is no way to restore a firm texture to a pickle that has already gone soft, there are ways to slant the odds of achieving the crisp consistency you're after in your favor.

The single most important thing is the quality of the ingredients you start out with. A limp cucumber cannot, ever, turn into a crunchy pickle. So always start out with firm, unblemished vegetables or fruit for the best pickles. This usually means younger and smaller vegetables. If you have less-than-perfect produce to work with, opt for a finely chopped or pureed recipe such as a chutney, relish, or ketchup rather than pickling large pieces of food.

Jam and Jelly Troubles

JELLY DOESN'T GEL OR JAM ISN'T THICK ENOUGH

Jelly and jam need the magic triad of sugar, pectin, and acid in order to achieve the gelled-but-spreadable consistency we expect from them. If any one of these elements is insufficient, you could still eventually arrive at an acceptable texture by boiling the ingredients until enough moisture evaporates out, but the long cooking time would eliminate much of the fruit flavor and color from the final product.

If your jelly or jam didn't gel despite reaching the sheet test or wrinkle test stage (see the Sweet Preserves chapter), there are a few possible reasons. One is that you decided to skimp on sugar and skimped a little too much. Another possibility is that there wasn't sufficient pectin: Low-pectin fruit needs a boost in order to achieve a gel (the Sweet Preserves chapter lists which fruits are high or low pectin). Still another possibility is that there wasn't sufficient acid, either from the main-ingredient fruit or from added lemon juice. And yet another possibility is that you didn't bring the mixture to a full, rolling boil and let it boil over high heat for at least a minute.

One solution is to reboil the food for 5 to 10 minutes. Another is to add an additional cup of sugar plus ½ cup of homemade pectin and reboil for an additional 2 to 5 minutes.

Yet another solution is to fix the runny jam or jelly by adding commercial pectin and a few other ingredients. To do this, first measure the preserves that need fixing. Then, for each quart of jam or jelly, add either 2 tablespoons commercial liquid pectin, 3/4 cup sugar, and 2 tablespoons bottled lemon juice; or 4 teaspoons commercial powdered pectin, 1/4 cup sugar, 2 tablespoons bottled lemon juice, and 1/4 cup water. Either way, stir the additional ingredients into the preserve you want to thicken, bring the mixture to a rolling boil, and boil it for 1 minute before ladling into freshly sterilized canning jars, covering with new canning lids, and processing in a boiling water bath (see the Boiling Water Bath Canning chapter) for 5 minutes.

Jelly that is too thin can always be used as syrup. Just sayin'.

JAM OR JELLY IS TOO THICK

You overboiled, and once the result cooled in the

sealed jars it was closer to a thick block of fruit leather or a sticky, gooey syrup than the spreadable preserve you were after. Although there's no way to transform what you've got into that originally intended product, there are a couple of ways to still salvage a usable, even tasty result.

In many cultures, especially those in many European countries, there is something called a fruit "cheese." Basically, this is just a fruit jam or jelly or butter that has been cooked until it is relatively solid and sliceable once cooled. The quince paste in the Dehydrating chapter is similar to this sort of preserve. Try setting a jar of your overcooked preserve in a bowl of piping-hot water for a few minutes. If you can then slide it out in one cylindrical piece (maybe with a little help from a table knife swiped around the sides), then just call it fruit cheese and serve it with crackers and the other kind of cheese.

Or, once you've set the jars in hot water long enough to soften the contents and pry them out, recook the preserve with a little water. It will never be jam or jelly, but you can turn it into usable syrup this way.

Dehydrated Food Dilemmas

MOISTURE CONDENSES ON THE INSIDES OF CONTAINERS OF DEHYDRATED FOOD, OR YOU SEE THE GREENISH WHITE FUZZ OF MOLD ON SOME OF THE FOOD

If the containers were completely dry when the dehydrated food went in, and if they were tightly sealed, then the only possible explanation is that the food wasn't dried well enough. If you catch this within a day or two of putting the not-quite-dried food into the containers, and if there are no signs of mold, you can fix the problem by simply returning the food to the dehydrator or oven, using the temperature originally specified for drying that type of food. How much additional drying time the food will need depends on how under-dehydrated it was in the first place. Make sure that you can see no beads of moisture form along the break line when you snap a piece of the food in half.

If the food was fully dehydrated, maybe even crispy-dry, and you see condensation on the insides of the container, then moisture got in from outside. Probably the container wasn't tightly enough sealed.

Here are two suggestions for avoiding moisture problems with dehydrated foods:

- Take the time for the conditioning step with dried fruits and vegetables. This is the step in which you fill a jar only two-thirds full and shake it daily for a week before finally transferring the food to fully filled containers (see individual ingredient instructions for specifics). This not only redistributes any residual moisture in the food, but also gives you a chance to spot early on whether the food needs additional drying time.

- Store dehydrated food, at least during that initial conditioning period, in transparent containers. Although I am a fan of stainless-steel food storage containers, with recently dehydrated food it is essential to spot even the scantest fog of moisture before mold becomes an issue. Since you can't see that through an opaque container, and clear, solid plastic presents its own problems (BPA health risks, for starters), glass is the way to go.

"MY CELERY LOOKS LIKE STRAW": WHY DRIED FOOD LOSES COLOR

If your bright green celery turned hay-beige once dehydrated, and your once orange carrots turned a weird sort of pale clay color, there are two things that could have gone wrong.

The first is that you ignored the blanching instructions in the Dehydrating chapter. Although some foods can be dehydrated without first being blanched, many will lose their color in storage unless you take the time for that "extra" step.

The second thing is that you stored your dried vegetables or fruits in a place where they were exposed to a lot of light or heat, like next to your radiator or in a sunny window.

So . . . do pay attention to those blanch-before-drying instructions, and don't store dried foods near direct light or heat.

"Can I Still Eat This?" Freezer, Fridge, and Cold Storage Spoilage

FREEZER BURN

Freezer burn occurs when moisture in the food evaporates into the freezer or into the air surrounding the food in a freezer container. It appears as a frost on the surface of the food, and causes whitish discolorations on the food. Although it isn't dangerous, freezer burn adversely affects the taste and texture of food, and can give it off odors.

The two main causes of freezer burn are storing food in the freezer too long and not packaging it well enough. There's really nothing you can do about the first problem except label and date everything that you put in to the freezer, and use up the oldest items first. To package food well for freezing, you need to minimize its exposure to air. That includes air inside sealed freezer bags and containers. Vacuum sealing will prevent freezer burn for the longest amount of time, but simply pressing the air out of bags and wrapping meats well will help significantly.

ROTTING IN COLD STORAGE (INCLUDING YOUR REFRIGERATOR)

Remember that cold storage delays spoilage, sometimes for months, but cannot actually eliminate it. Always remove any food showing signs of rotting so that it doesn't speed the spoilage of the rest of the food. Aside from simply having been in storage for too long, or being exposed to an already rotting fruit or vegetable, the most likely reason that food spoiled faster than it should have in cold storage is that it was improperly stored to begin with. See the Cold Storage chapter for specifics on how to correctly store food in your refrigerator or root cellar.

Approximate pH Values of Various Foods

Knowing the pH values of different ingredients will help you determine which of the canning methods in this book are safe. Remember that boiling water bath canning requires the food to have a pH of 4.6 or lower. All food with a pH higher than 4.6 needs to be pressure canned, unless you lower its pH by increasing its acidity sufficiently, as is done with vinegar pickled vegetables.

Apples 3.30–4.00
Apple juice 3.35–4.00
Applesauce 3.10–3.60
Apricots 3.30–4.80
Artichokes. 5.50–6.00
Artichokes, Jerusalem 5.93–6.00
Asparagus. 6.00–6.70
Bamboo shoots. 5.10–6.20
Beans 5.60–6.50
Beans, green and wax. 5.30–5.70
Beets 5.30–6.60
Blackberries. 3.85–4.50
Blueberries 3.12–3.33
Broccoli. 5.20–6.00
Brussels sprouts 6.00–6.30

Buttermilk. 4.41–4.83
Cabbage 5.20–6.80
Calamari (squid) 5.80
Cantaloupe 6.13–6.58
Carp. 6.00
Carrots 5.88–6.40
Cauliflower 5.60
Celery. 5.70–6.00
Chayote (mirliton). 6.00–6.30
Cherries 3.25–3.83
Chicory. 5.90–6.05
Clams. 6.00–7.10
Coconut, fresh 5.50–7.80
Coconut milk 6.10–7.00
Codfish. 5.30–6.10
Corn. 5.90–7.30
Crabmeat 6.50–7.00
Cranberry juice. 2.30–2.52
Cream. 6.50–6.68
Cucumbers 5.12–5.78
Cuttlefish. 6.30
Dates 4.14–4.88
Eggplant. 5.50–6.50
Eggs. 6.58
Eel 6.20
Escarole 5.70–6.00
Fennel 5.48–5.88

Figs	5.05–5.98	Maple syrup	5.15
Flounder	6.10–6.90	Melon	.5.78–6.67
Garlic	5.80	Milk	6.40–6.80
Ginger	5.60–5.90	Molasses	4.90–5.40
Gooseberries	2.80–3.10	Mushrooms	6.00–6.70
Grapes	2.80–3.80	Mussels	6.00–6.85
Grapefruit	3.00–3.75	Mustard	3.55–6.00
Greens, mixed, chopped	5.05–5.22	Nectarines	.3.92–4.18
Guava, canned	.3.37–4.10	Octopus	6.00–6.50
Haddock	.6.17–6.82	Okra	5.50–6.60
Hearts of palm	.5.70	Onion	5.30–5.85
Herring	6.10	Oranges	3.69–4.34
Honey	3.70–4.20	Orange juice	.3.30–4.19
Horseradish, freshly ground	5.35	Oysters	.5.68–6.17
Huckleberries	.3.38–3.43	Papaya	5.20–6.00
Kale, cooked	6.36–6.80	Parsnip	5.30–5.70
Kelp	.6.30	Pâté	.5.90
Kumquat	.3.64–4.25	Peaches	3.30–4.05
Leeks	.5.50–6.17	Pears	3.50–4.60
Lemon juice	2.00–2.60	Peas, chick (garbanzo beans), cooked	6.48–6.80
Lentils, cooked	6.30–6.83	Peas, dried (split green), cooked	6.45–6.80
Lettuce	.5.80–6.15	Peas, dried (split yellow), cooked	6.43–6.62
Lime juice	2.00–2.35	Peas	4.90–6.70
Lime	2.00–2.80	Peppers	.4.65–5.45
Lobster	.7.10–7.43	Persimmons	4.42–4.70
Loganberries	2.70–3.50	Pineapple	3.20–4.00
Loquat	5.10	Pineapple juice	3.30–3.60
Lotus root	.6.90	Plums	2.80–4.45
Lychee	.4.70–5.01	Potatoes	5.40–5.90
Mackerel	5.90–6.40	Prunes (dried plums)	.3.63–3.92
Mangoes, ripe	3.40–4.80	Pumpkin	4.90–5.50
Mangoes, green	5.80–6.00		

Quince	.3.12–3.40	Strawberries	3.00–3.90
Radishes	5.52–6.05	Sweet potatoes	5.30–5.60
Raisins	3.80–4.10	Swiss chard	.6.17–6.78
Raspberries	.3.22–3.95	Tamarind	.3.00
Rhubarb	.3.10–3.40	Tangerine	.3.32–4.48
Salmon	5.85–6.50	Tofu	.7.20
Sardines	5.70–6.60	Tomatillo	.3.83
Sauerkraut	3.30–3.60	Tomatoes	4.30–4.90
Scallion	.6.20	Trout	6.20–6.33
Scallop	.6.00	Truffle	5.30–6.50
Shad roe	5.70–5.90	Turnips	5.29–5.90
Shallots	5.30–5.70	Turnip greens	5.40–6.20
Shrimp	6.50–7.00	Vegetable juice	3.90–4.30
Spinach	5.50–6.80	Water chestnut	6.00–6.20s
Squash, winter	.5.18–6.49	Watercress	.5.88–6.18
Squash, summer, including		Watermelon	.5.18–5.60
zucchini	5.79–6.00	Yams	.5.50–6.81
Sturgeon	.6.20		

WEBSITES

Food Preservation at About.com (foodpreservation.about.com)

This is my food preservation site. There are hundreds of recipes here as well as articles on everything from lacto-fermentation to the history of canning and how to safely make and use homemade vinegar in pickling. I am constantly adding to the site, so although you've got all of the core information here in this book, there are already new recipes online.

Garden Fork TV (gardenfork.tv)

Eric Rochow has a plethora of DIY videos here, and many of them are on making different kinds of preserved foods. His instructions are clear, fun, and accurate.

Hunter, Angler, Gardener, Cook (honest-food.net)

This is Hank Shaw's site, and lots of the recipes and advice on it pertain to food preservation. I trust his recipes absolutely. If you're especially interested in ways to preserve wild game meats, this website is for you.

Leda's Urban Homestead Videos (youtube.com/ledameredith)

If you want to get into the kitchen with me and have more visuals to augment the information in this book, here is where you'll find short videos (under five minutes) of me cooking, foraging, and preserving food.

National Center for Home Food Preservation (nchfp.uga.edu)

The information on this site is regularly updated to reflect the latest scientific information on safe food preservation. I'm not too crazy about the recipes, to be honest, but if you just need to quickly look up a canning time or other technical info (and don't have this book handy), this is the site I would go to.

Wild Fermentation (wildfermentation.com)

Sandor Ellix Katz is the best-known expert on every kind of fermentation from the lacto-fermentation described in this book to homebrewing, sourdough baking, kombucha maintainance, and more. If you want to delve deeper into the culinary realm of working with the beneficial bacteria we share the planet with, you'll definitely want to spend time on this site.

BOOKS

Charcuterie: The Craft of Salting, Smoking, and Curing by Michael Ruhlman and Brian Polcyn

This is the book that took the mystery out of safely and deliciously curing meats, and thus returned those skills to the home cook.

The Complete Root Cellar Book by Steve Maxwell and Jennifer MacKenzie

A great source for clear, easy-to-follow and -build root cellar designs.

Making Wild Wines and Meads by Pattie Vargas and Rich Gulling

If you want to delve deeper into making your own wines (and meads, which are honey-based wines) at home, this book is a great starting point. The recipes are for 1-gallon batches, which makes them reasonable for the home-brewer with limited space. The wild in the title refers to the fact that a number of the recipes are meant to be made with foraged wild edible fruits, flowers, and herbs.

Nourishing Traditions: The Cookbook That Challenges Politically Correct Nutrition and the Diet Dictocrats by Sally Fallon

In this book, Sally Fallon debunks the idea that animal fats are health evils, as well as thoroughly explaining the health benefits of fermented foods. She includes numerous recipes and instructions for incorporating these time-tested ingredients into your diet.

Preserving Food Without Freezing or Canning: Traditional Techniques Using Salt, Oil, Sugar, Alcohol, Vinegar, Drying, Cold Storage, and Lactic Fermentation by the Farmers and Gardeners of Terre Vivante

As the title says, there's not a single canning recipe in this book, nor a word about frozen foods. Instead, these are low-tech, time-tested food preservation recipes and methods from gardeners and farmers in France. One of the main intentions of this book was to preserve these ways of keeping food fresh before they were lost from memory. I've tried almost every recipe in the book, and they deliver as promised.

Wild Fermentation and *The Art of Fermentation* by Sandor Ellix Katz

These two books by fermentation expert Sandor Ellix Katz cover not only the simple lacto-fermented foods like yogurt and sauerkraut that I've included here, but also other fermented foods: homebrewed alcohols, homemade miso, and many others. Sandor's books go into great detail on the hows and whys of the biological activity that makes fermentation happen, and also include many excellent recipes.

GEAR

Canning Jars, Lids, Jar Lifters, and Other Canning Gear

You can find most of these at hardware stores and kitchen supply stores, and you can also find good deals sometimes in thrift shops or yard sales (just remember to carefully inspect canning jars for cracks before you use them). There are numerous online sites to order from; one I like a lot is Lehman's (lehmans.com).

Crocks

The Schmitt Fermenting Crock is, in my opinion, the Rolls-Royce of fermentation crocks. Not because it is high tech or fancy: quite the opposite. But it is elegantly and efficiently designed, and does its job well. The design is based on one that used to be offered by the Harsch company. The main body of the crock is a ceramic cylinder, the same as any crock. But around the rim is a built-in moat that you fill with water. Two semi-circular pieces fit into the cylinder and act as weights to hold the food being fermented under the brine. And a lid that has a couple of cutaways sits in the moat of water. The water in the moat prevents air, molds, and so forth from getting into the crock. The cutaways in the lid allow the gases produced by fermentation to escape. You can get Schmitt Fermenting Crocks from The Canning Pantry (canningpantry.com), as well as lots of other food preservation gear.

Dehydrators

Excalibur (excaliburdehydrator.com) makes excellent dehydrators that range from a small four-tray economy model to huge stainless-steel commercial models. The Excalibur dehydrators are my first choice, but NESCO's (nesco.com/products/Dehydrators) models are also good. Both companies offer accessories, recipes, and information on dehydrated foods on their websites.

Pressure Canners

Two brands that I especially recommend are Presto (gopresto.com) and All-American (allamericancanner.com). Both sites offer canning supplies in addition to canners, and the Presto site also has complete manuals for each of its canner models available for download.

Tattler Reusable, BPA-Free Canning Lids (reusablecanninglids.com)

These lids come in both regular and widemouth sizes and work with standard canning jars and rings. But unlike the central disks of conventional two-piece canning lids, Tattler lids can be used over and over for years. They are definitely pricier than conventional lids when you first buy them, but quickly pay for themselves if you reuse them as often as I do. Also, the plastic they are made with is BPA-free, unlike the plastic coating on the underside of conventional canning lids.

Acid Titration Test Kits, Wine Yeast, Yeast Nutrient, Fermentation Locks, and More . . .

These can be ordered from home winemaking companies. I especially like Grapestompers, thanks to its excellent customer service (grapestompers.com). If you order an acid titration kit from Grapestompers (or any other company), remember that the instructions (given in the Vinegar Pickling chapter) for testing the acetic acid percentage of homemade vinegar are different from the wine testing instructions that come with the kit.

Hygrometers and pH Meters (digital-meters.com)

You can get both devices from Digital Meters.

Vacuum Sealers (foodsaver.com)

Food Saver has several kinds of vacuum sealers including inexpensive handheld models and sturdier tabletop versions.

BPA-Free Food Storage and Freezer Containers (lifewithoutplastic.com)

Because of the health concerns over harmful BPAs released into food by many types of plastic food containers, I recommend switching to BPA-free alternatives. The food containers sold by Life Without Plastic are not only BPA-free but also very sturdy, freezer safe, and elegantly designed.

INGREDIENTS

Low-Methoxyl Pectin (pomonapectin.com)

Pomona's Universal Pectin is the brand I use for no- and low-sugar jellies and jams. It is a small, family-operated business that offers a good product and excellent service: The folks there are happy to help you with any questions.

Curing Salts, Citric Acid, and Spices (thespicehouse.com)

The Spice House has good-quality spices—including pink curing salt #1 (also called Prague Powder #1), which is the curing salt used in the preserved meat recipes in this book. The company also carries citric acid.

Rennet, Cheese Starter Cultures, Butter Muslin (cheesemaking.com)

Not only does New England Home Cheesemaking Supply sell everything you need to make the simple cheese recipes I've shared, it also has kits that can get you started with more advanced cheese-making projects like aged hard cheeses.

Note: Page references in *italics* indicate recipe photographs.

A

Acetic acid, testing for, 85
Acid titration test kit, 15, 85
Alcohol. *See* Preserving in Alcohol
Apple(s)
    Pectin, Homemade, 92–93
    Salsa, Fermented, 46–47
    Scrap Jelly, 100–101, *101*
    Scrap Vinegar, 86–87
    Stovetop Applesauce, 54–55, *55*
Applesauce, Stovetop, 54–55, *55*
Artichokes, blanching before freezing, 188
Ascorbic acid crystals, 142
Asparagus
    blanching, before dehydrating, 153
    blanching, before freezing, 188
    pressure canning, 125
Avocados, freezing, 193

B

Bacon, 179–80
Bacteria, beneficial, 21–22
Bacteria, lethal, 22
Baked goods, freezing, 186
Basil oil, freezing, 190–91

Beans. *See also* Green Beans
    blanching, before dehydrating, 153
    blanching, before freezing, 188
    dry rehydrated, pressure canning, 125–26
    freezer shelf life, 186
    freshly shelled, pressure canning, 127
    wax, pressure canning, 126
Beets
    blanching, before dehydrating, 153
    Naturally Pink Cauliflower Pickles, 76–77
    pressure canning, 127
Berries. *See also* Cranberry(ies)
    boiling water bath canning, 62
    freezing, 189
    Raspberry Cordial, 244–45, *245*
    Strawberry Jam, 98–99
Blueberries, boiling water bath canning, 62
Boiling Water Bath Canning, 48–62
    blanched and peeled method for tomatoes, 58–59
    blueberries and other berries, 62

food safety considerations, 48–49
gear for, 13–15, 49
high-acid foods for, 48–49
high altitude adjustments, 56
history of, 48
hot pack method for tomatoes, 58
how it works, 49
how to can tomatoes, 57
how to sterilize jars, 50
loading the jars, 50
peaches and other fruits, 60–61
pressure canner used as boiling water bath, 137
processing jars in the boiling water bath, 53
raw pack method for tomatoes, 57–58
roasting method for tomatoes, 58–59
setting up the canning equipment, 49–50
Stovetop Applesauce, 54–55, *55*
troubleshooting, 252–53
unsafe methods, 52
when to sterilize jars, 50
Botulism, 122
Bourbon, Kumquat Marmalade with, 108–9, *109*
Brandied or Fermented Sour Cherries, 250–51, *251*

Brandied Peaches, 238–39, *239*
Bread-and-Butter Pickles, 72–73, *73*
Brine
    appearance of, 24
    keeping food submerged in, 29
    leftover, uses for, 28
    role of, in fermentation, 22
Broccoli, blanching before freezing, 188
Brussels sprouts
    blanching, before dehydrating, 153
    blanching, before freezing, 188
Butcher paper, 18
Butter. *See also* Preserving in Oil, Butter, and Other Fats
    Herb, 230–31, *231*

C

Cabbage
    blanching, before dehydrating, 153
    Radish Kimchi, 35–37
    Single-Jar Sauerkraut, 30–33, *31*
Candied Grapefruit Peels, 116–19, *117*
Canning funnel, 13
Canning jars and lids, 13–14
    checking the seals, 53
    filled, cooling down, 53

filling, for boiling water bath canning, 50
how and when to sterilize, 50
processing, for boiling water bath canning, 53
Carrots
blanching, before dehydrating, 153
Giardinieri: Mixed Italian Antipasto Garden Pickle, 198–200, *199*
pressure canning, 127–28
Cauliflower
blanching, before dehydrating, 153
blanching, before freezing, 188
Giardinieri: Mixed Italian Antipasto Garden Pickle, 198–200, *199*
Pickles, Naturally Pink, 76–77
Celery
blanching, before dehydrating, 153
Giardinieri: Mixed Italian Antipasto Garden Pickle, 198–200, *199*
Ceramic crock, 13
Charcoal chimney, 17
Chard, Fermented, 26–27
Cheesecloth or butter muslin, 19
Cheese making
best milk for, 206
Feta Cheese, *216*, 217–19
gear for, 19
how to make yogurt cheese, 211

Queso Blanco/Paneer Cheese, 214–15, *215*
Ricotta Cheese, 212–13, *213*
Cherry(ies)
Sour, Brandied or Fermented, 250–51, *251*
Syrup, 110–11, *111*
Cherry pitter, 10
Chutney
Green Tomato, 78–79
ten ways to use, 80–81
Citric acid, 142
Citrus Pectin, Homemade, 94–95
The "Clamp," 205
Clostridium botulinum, 120
Cold Storage, 194–205
best refrigerator practices, 196
gear for, 18
Giardinieri: Mixed Italian Antipasto Garden Pickle, 198–200, *199*
how it works, 194–95
root cellaring, 201–5
troubleshooting, 258
where to store what in refrigerator, 195–96
Confit, Duck, 225–26, *227*
"Confit" Vegetables, 228–29
Conserves, description of, 88
Container cellars, 203–5
Corn
blanching, before dehydrating, 153
pressure canning, 128–29
Cornichon Pickles, 70–71, *71*
Cranberry(ies)
Dried, *144*, 144–45
how to dry in a dehydrator, 143

Sauce, Jellied, with Spicebush and Orange, 106–7, *107*
Cucumber(s)
Bread-and-Butter Pickles, 72–73, *73*
Cornichon Pickles, 70–71, *71*
Quick Refrigerator Dill Pickles, 66–67
and Red Pepper Relish, Sweet, 83–84
Curd, Lemon, 114–15, *115*
Curing process, 174
Curing salts, about, 174

D

Dairy cultures. *See* Cheese making; Yogurt
Dandelion Wine, 248–49
Deep pot, 15
Dehydrating, 140–67
air-drying green beans, 162
in a dehydrator, 141
Dehydrator Method Kale Chips the Quick Way, 156–57
Dehydrator Method Kale Chips the Raw Food Way, 158–59
Dried Cranberries, *144*, 144–45
Dried Green Beans, 160–61
fruit, 142–43
Fruit Leather, 146–47
gear for, 17
herbs, 162–63
history of, 140
Jerky from Ground Turkey, 165–67, *166*

meats, poultry, and fish, 164
mushrooms, 163–64
nutrients preserved by, 141
Oven Method Kale Chips, 154–55
Quince Paste, 148–50, *149*
tomatoes, 151–52
troubleshooting, 257–58
vegetables, 151–53
Dehydrator, 17
Dial gauge pressure canner, 16
Digital meat thermometer, 17
Dill Pickles, Quick Refrigerator, 66–67
Dilly Beans, 74–75
Duck Confit, 225–26, *227*

E

Eggplant
blanching, before dehydrating, 153
Ratatouille with Roasted Vegetables, 138–39
Eggs, freezing, 189
Elderflower Champagne, 246–47, *247*
Equipment
for boiling water bath canning, 13–15, 49
for cold storage, 18
for dehydrating, 17
for freezing, 17–18
generally useful gear, 10–12
for lacto-fermentation, 12–13
for preserving in alcohol, 19

for pressure canning,
13–15, 16
for salting and smoking,
17
for simple cheese
making, 19
for sweet preserves, 13–16
for vinegar pickling,
13–15

F
Fermentation lock, 19
Fermented Apple Salsa, 46–47
Fermented Chard, 26–27
Fermented foods. *See* Lacto-
fermentation
Feta Cheese, *216*, 217–19
Fig Preserves with Wine and
Balsamic Vinegar, 104–5,
105
Fish
dehydrating, 164
freezer shelf life, 187
freezing, 189–90
pressure canning, 135
Salt, 172–73
Smoked Trout, 181–83,
182
Food mill, 16
Food processor, 10
Food safety
boiling water bath
canning, 48–49
learning about, 9
unsafe boiling water bath
canning methods,
52
Freezer bags and/or
containers, 17–18
Freezing, 184–93
avocados, 193
basil oil, 190–91
berries, 189

blanching foods prior to,
188–89
chopped ingredients, 189
cooked leftovers, 192–93
eggs, 189
freezer shelf life of foods,
186–87
fresh ginger, 192
gear for, 17–18
how it preserves food
safely, 184
leafy greens, 191–92
meat, poultry, and
seafood, 189–90
minimizing quality
decline, 184–85
packing freezer full for,
185
refreezing foods, note
about, 185
Fruit. *See also specific fruits*
best, for cellaring, 202
candied, preparing, 119
canned, making fruit
leathers from, 147
dehydrating, 142–43
fermenting, 45
float and discoloration,
solutions for, 254–55
freezer shelf life, 186
high-acid, for boiling
water bath canning,
48–49
hot pack boiling water
bath canning, 60–61
Leather, 146–47
Pemmican, 234–35, *235*
Rumtopf, 240–41, *241*
selecting, for lacto-
fermentation, 28
Fruit butters
description of, 88
how to make, 103

Slow-Cooker Pear Butter,
102–3
Spiced Pear Butter, 103
Spiked Pear Butter, 103

G
Gel point, judging, 96–97
Giardinieri: Mixed Italian
Antipasto Garden Pickle,
198–200, *199*
Ginger, freezing, 192
Grains, freezer shelf life,
186
Grapefruit Peels, Candied,
116–19, *117*
Green Beans
air-drying, 162
blanching, before
dehydrating, 153
blanching before
freezing, 188
Dilly Beans, 74–75
Dried, 160–61
Lacto-Fermented, 38–40,
39
pressure canning, 126
Greens
blanching, before
dehydrating, 153
blanching, before
freezing, 188
blanching and freezing,
191–92
Dehydrator Method Kale
Chips the Quick Way,
156–57
Dehydrator Method Kale
Chips the Raw Food
Way, 158–59
Fermented Chard, 26–27
Oven Method Kale
Chips, 154–55
Green Tomato Chutney, 78–79

H
Herb(s)
blanching before
freezing, 188
Butter, 230–31, *231*
drying, 162–63
salts, making, 169
High altitude adjustments
for boiling water bath
canning, 56
for pressure canning, 123
Hygrometer, 18

J
Jams
description of, 88
Strawberry, 98–99
troubleshooting, 256–57
Jar lifter, 14
Jars
breaking, while
processing, 254
failing to seal, 252–53
fruit floats and
discoloration, 254–55
Jelly
Apple Scrap, 100–101, *101*
description of, 88
how to make, 99
troubleshooting, 256–57
Jelly bag, 15–16, 19
Jerky from Ground Turkey,
165–67, *166*

K
Kale Chips
Dehydrator Method, the
Quick Way, 156–57
Dehydrator Method, the
Raw Food Way, 158–59
Oven Method, 154–55
Kimchi, Radish, 35–37
Kitchen scale, 10–11

Kumquat Marmalade with Bourbon, 108–9, *109*

L

Labneh (Yogurt Cheese), 211
Lactic acid, 22
Lactobacillus, 22, 24, 25, 45, 206, 210
Lacto-fermentation, 21–47
  adding starter culture, 24–25
  commonly known foods, 21
  Fermented Apple Salsa, 46–47
  Fermented Chard, 26–27
  Fermented Hot Chile Pepper Sauce, 42–44
  fermenting fruit, 45
  gear for, 12–13
  history of, 21
  how it preserves food safely, 22
  Lacto-Fermented Green Beans, 38–40, *39*
  making big-batch recipes, 29
  with only filtered water, 25
  popularity of, 21–22
  Radish Kimchi, 35–37
  salt-free ferments, notes about, 24–25, 28
  serving ideas for fermented vegetables, 41
  Single-Jar Sauerkraut, 30–33, *31*
  storing ferments, 28
  successful, tips for, 28–29
  troubleshooting, 252
  using fermented foods in cooked recipes, 29

what to expect during fermentation, 24
Leftovers
  freezer shelf life, 186–87
  freezing, tips for, 192–93
Lemon(s)
  Curd, 114–15, *115*
  juice treatment, for dehydrating, 142
  Limoncello, 242–43, *243*
  Moroccan-Style Preserved, 170–71, *171*
Lid lifter, 14–15
Limoncello, 242–43, *243*
Live cultures, 22

M

Mandoline, 11
Marmalade
  description of, 88
  Kumquat, with Bourbon, 108–9, *109*
  thickening, over time, 108
Meat. *See also* Pork
  dehydrating, 164
  freezer shelf life, 187
  freezing, 189–90
  Pemmican, 234–35, *235*
  pressure canning, 132–33
Milk. *See* Cheese making; Yogurt
Moroccan-Style Preserved Lemons, 170–71, *171*
Mortar and pestle, 12
Mushrooms
  Antipasto Marinated, 222–24
  drying, 163–64
  freezer shelf life, 187
  pressure canning, 129

N

Nitrates and nitrites, 174
Nuts, freezer shelf life, 187

O

Oil. *See also* Preserving in Oil, Butter, and Other Fats
  basil, freezing, 190–91
  Rosemary, 232–33
Okra
  blanching, before dehydrating, 153
  blanching, before freezing, 188
  pressure canning, 129–30
Onions, blanching, before dehydrating, 153
Orange and Spicebush, Jellied Cranberry Sauce with, 106–7, *107*

P

Pancetta, 176–77
Paneer/Queso Blanco Cheese, 214–15, *215*
Parsnips, blanching, before dehydrating, 153
Peaches
  Brandied, 238–39, *239*
  hot pack boiling water bath canning, 60–61
Pear Butter
  Slow-Cooker, 102–3
  Spiced, 103
  Spiked, 103
Peas
  blanching, before dehydrating, 153
  blanching, before freezing, 189
  pressure canning, 130
Pectin
  Apple, Homemade, 92–93

Citrus, Homemade, 94–95
  fruits high in, 91
  fruits low in, 91
  for low- or no-sugar preserves, 90
Pemmican, 234–35, *235*
Pepper(s)
  chile, blanching, before dehydrating, 153
  Giardinieri: Mixed Italian Antipasto Garden Pickle, 198–200, *199*
  Hot Chile, Fermented, Sauce, 42–44
  Ratatouille with Roasted Vegetables, 138–39
  Red, and Cucumber Relish, Sweet, 83–84
  sweet, blanching, before dehydrating, 153
  sweet, pressure canning, 131
  Whole Chile, Pickled, 68–69, *69*
pH meters, 15, 64
pH values
  of sugar, 88
  of various foods, 259–61
Pickles
  Bread-and-Butter, 72–73, *73*
  canned vinegar, about, 64–65
  Cauliflower, Naturally Pink, 76–77
  Cornichon, 70–71, *71*
  Dill, Quick Refrigerator, 66–67
  Dilly Beans, 74–75
  Giardinieri: Mixed Italian Antipasto

Garden Pickle, 198–200, *199*

Pickled Whole Chile Peppers, 68–69, *69*

refrigerator, about, 64, 197

refrigerator, vegetables for, 67

sweet-and-sour, about, 65

Pork

  Bacon, 179–80

  Pancetta, 176–77

Potatoes, blanching, before dehydrating, 153

Poultry. *See also* Turkey

  dehydrating, 164

  freezer shelf life, 187

  freezing, 189–90

  pressure canning, 133–34

Preserving in Alcohol, 237–51

  Brandied or Fermented Sour Cherries, 250–51, *251*

  Brandied Peaches, 238–39, *239*

  Dandelion Wine, 248–49

  Elderflower Champagne, 246–47, *247*

  gear for, 19

  how it works, 237

  Limoncello, 242–43, *243*

  Raspberry Cordial, 244–45, *245*

  Rumtopf, 240–41, *241*

Preserving in Oil, Butter, and Other Fats, 221–35

  Antipasto Marinated Mushrooms, 222–24

  "Confit" Vegetables, 228–29

  Duck Confit, 225–26, *227*

  Herb Butter, 230–31, *231*

  how it works, 221

Pemmican, 234–35, *235*

Rosemary Oil, 232–33

Pressure canners

  description of, 122

  how to use, 122–24

  using as a boiling water bath, 137

Pressure Canning, 120–39

  fish, 135

  gear for, 13–15, *16*

  high altitude adjustments, 123

  meat, 132–33

  multi-ingredient recipes, 136

  poultry, 133–34

  rabbit, 134–35

  Ratatouille with Roasted Vegetables, 138–39

  shellfish, 135–36

  soup stocks, 132

  troubleshooting, 252–53

  vegetables, 124–31

  when it is necessary, 120–22

  working with pressure canners, 122–24

Probiotics, 21. *See also* Lactobacillus

  effect of heat on, 29

  in starter cultures, 24–25

Pumpkin, pressure canning, 131

Q

Queso Blanco/Paneer Cheese, 214–15, *215*

Quince Paste, 148–50, *149*

R

Rabbit, pressure canning, 134–35

Radish Kimchi, 35–37

Raspberry Cordial, 244–45, *245*

Ratatouille with Roasted Vegetables, 138–39

Refrigerator pickles

  about, 64, 197

  vegetables for, 67

Relish, Sweet Red Pepper and Cucumber, 83–84

Ricotta Cheese, 212–13, *213*

Root cellaring, 201–5

Rosemary Oil, 232–33

Round rack, 15

Rumtopf, 240–41, *241*

S

Salsa, Fermented Apple, 46–47

Salting and Smoking, 168–83

  Bacon, 179–80

  cold-smoking process, 174

  curing process, 174

  drying after curing and before smoking, 175

  dry salting, description of, 169

  gear for, 17

  hot-smoking process, 174

  Moroccan-Style Preserved Lemons, 170–71, *171*

  Pancetta, 176–77

  Salt Fish, 172–73

  salting versus smoking, 168

  Smoked Trout, 181–83, *182*

  smokers for, 174–75

Salt(s)

  curing, about, 174

  effect on lacto-fermentation, 24

-free ferments, notes about, 24–25, 28

herb, making, 169

Sauces

  Fermented Hot Chile Pepper, 42–44

  Jellied Cranberry, with Spicebush and Orange, 106–7, *107*

Sauerkraut, Single-Jar, 30–33, *31*

Shellfish

  freezer shelf life, 187

  freezing, 189–90

  pressure canning, 135–36

Slotted spoon, 12

Smokers, 17, 174–75

Smoking. *See* Salting and Smoking

Soup stocks

  freezer shelf life, 187

  pressure canning, 132

Spicebush and Orange, Jellied Cranberry Sauce with, 106–7, *107*

Spiced Pear Butter, 103

Spiked Pear Butter, 103

Squash

  blanching, before dehydrating, 153

  blanching, before freezing, 189

  Ratatouille with Roasted Vegetables, 138–39

  winter, pressure canning, 131

Stainless-steel containers, 19

Starter cultures

  definition of, 24–25

  making your own, 25

  whey, from yogurt, 24

Strawberry Jam, 98–99

Sugar
  low- or no-sugar
    preserves, 90
  pH of, 88
  role in sweet preserves,
    89
Sweet-and-sour pickle
  recipes, about, 65
Sweet Preserves, 88–119
  Apple Scrap Jelly, 100–
    101, *101*
  Candied Grapefruit
    Peels, 116–19, *117*
  Cherry Syrup, 110–11, *111*
  Fig Preserves with Wine
    and Balsamic Vinegar,
    104–5, *105*
  gear for, 13–16
  high- and low-pectin fruit
    for, 91
  Homemade Apple Pectin,
    92–93
  Homemade Citrus
    Pectin, 94–95
  Jellied Cranberry Sauce
    with Spicebush and
    Orange, 106–7, *107*
  judging gel point, 96–97
  Kumquat Marmalade
    with Bourbon, 108–9,
    109
  Lemon Curd, 114–15, *115*
  making low- or no-sugar
    preserves, 90
  Slow-Cooker Pear Butter,
    102–3
  Spiced Pear Butter, 103
  Spiked Pear Butter, 103
  Strawberry Jam, 98–99

troubleshooting, 256–57
types of, 88
Violet Flower Syrup,
  112–13, *113*
what makes them safe,
  88–89
Syrups
  Cherry, 110–11, *111*
  description of, 88
  Violet Flower, 112–13, *113*

T
Thermometer, 19
Tomato(es)
  blanched and peeled
    canning method,
    58–59
  boiling water bath
    canning, 57
  dehydrating, 151–52
  Green, Chutney, 78–79
  hot pack method, 58
  Ratatouille with Roasted
    Vegetables, 138–39
  raw pack method, 57–58
  roasted canning method,
    59
Troubleshooting
  canning, 252–55
  cold storage, 258
  dehydrating, 257–58
  jams and jellies, 256–57
  lacto-fermentation, 252
  pickling, 255
Trout, Smoked, 181–83, *182*
Turkey
  Ground, Jerky from,
    165–67, *166*
  Pemmican, 234–35, *235*

V
Vacuum sealer, 18
Vegetables. *See also specific*
  vegetables
  best, for cellaring, 202
  "Confit," 228–29
  dehydrating, 151–53
  freezer shelf life, 187
  making refrigerator
    pickles with, 67
  selecting, for lacto-
    fermentation, 28
Vinegar
  Apple Scrap, 86–87
  Balsamic, and Wine, Fig
    Preserves with, 104–5,
    105
  best, for vinegar pickling,
    65
  homemade, for pickling
    recipes, 85
  testing for acetic acid, 85
Vinegar Pickling, 64–87
  Apple Scrap Vinegar,
    86–87
  best vinegars for, 65
  Bread-and-Butter Pickles,
    72–73, *73*
  canned vinegar pickles,
    about, 64–65
  Cornichon Pickles, 70–71,
    71
  Dilly Beans, 74–75
  gear for, 13–15
  Green Tomato Chutney,
    78–79
  Naturally Pink
    Cauliflower Pickles,
    76–77

Pickled Whole Chile
  Peppers, 68–69, *69*
Quick Refrigerator Dill
  Pickles, 66–67
refrigerator pickles,
  about, 64
sweet-and-sour pickle
  recipes, about, 65
Sweet Red Pepper and
  Cucumber Relish,
  83–84
troubleshooting, 255
Violet Flower Syrup, 112–13,
  113

W
Water, for lacto-fermentation,
  25
Weighted or dial gauge
  pressure canner, 16
Whey yogurt starter culture,
  24
Widemouth glass jars, 12–13,
  19
Wine, Dandelion, 248–49
Wine and Balsamic Vinegar,
  Fig Preserves with, 104–5,
  105

Y
Yogurt, 209–11
  cheese, how to make, 211
  how to make, 206
  plain, turning into Greek,
    211
  whey starter culture
    from, 24

ACKNOWLEDGMENTS

Thanks to:

My Brooklyn sustainable food system allies.
Whether you are still in BK, or have moved on to cooking,
foraging, and farming up a storm elsewhere, you were very
much my inspiration for sharing the information in this book:
Melissa Danielle, Valentina and Vasileas Galanis,
Jackie Gordon, Claudia Joseph, Stacey Murphy, Liz Neves,
Annie Novak, Megan Paska, Eric Rochow,
Jeremy and Allie Umansky.
Everyone at the Park Slope CSA, especially Tom Twente
and farmers Ted, Jan, Nancy, and Alan, for a decade of
wonderful food and community. And a shout-out to the
7:30 AM Sunday maintenance A squad at the Food Co-op.
Penelope and Frank Coberly, Anne Kochanski Gonzalez,
Stephanie Huffakker, Sam Householder, Kelly Johnson,
Richard Orbach, Francis Patrelle, Susan Pell, Natalie Waters,
and Ellen Zachos for having my back while I went through
an unexpected change of address and other upheavals
while typing away toward this book's deadline.
The editorial team at The Countryman Press for
suggesting this book in the first place, and then working
with me to make it awesome.

ABOUT THE AUTHOR

As the food preservation expert for About.com, Leda Meredith shares her passion for safe, delicious food preservation recipes and techniques at foodpreservation.about.com, as well as when she teaches the subject for the New York Botanical Garden, Just Food, Brooklyn Botanic Garden, Slow Food International, and numerous other organizations. Food preservation is also a frequent topic on her Leda's Urban Homestead blog (ledameredith.com) and video channel (youtube.com/ledameredith).

Leda is the author of three previous books, all of which feature food preservation recipes and information. *Botany, Ballet, & Dinner from Scratch: A Memoir with Recipes* (Heliotrope Books, 2008) is the story of how this former professional dancer ended up working at two botanical gardens and teaching foraging and food preservation skills. *The Locavore's Handbook: The Busy Person's Guide to Eating Local on a Budget* (Lyons Press, 2010) shares her tips for eating an environmentally friendly, local, organic diet in a cold winter climate with limited space, time, and cash. *Northeast Foraging: 120 Wild and Flavorful Plants from Beach Plums to Wineberries* (Timber Press, 2014) is a field guide to the wild edible plants of the Northeast that includes preservation tips for each plant.